From the Scythia to Sunderland

*

The golden life
of
Sir Tommy Steele

*

Richard R. Dolphin

ALSO BY RICHARD R. DOLPHIN:

COLLECTING BEER CANS

1977, Trewin Copplestone Publishing Ltd

THE INTERNATIONAL BOOK OF BEER CAN COLLECTING

1977, Hamlyn Publishing Group Ltd

4 impressions in UK and USA

FIRE POWER

1982 private publication by St Andrews Church, West Hatch

THE FUNDAMENTALS OF CORPORATE COMMUNICATIONS

1998, Butterworth-Heinemann

THROUGH ALL THE CHANGING SCENES OF LIFE

2018, Amazon

A PROUD PHOENIX FLEW OVER WEST HATCH

2019, Amazon

SWEET INSPIRATIONS

2019, Amazon

Richard Dolphin

is an author and lecturer:

based in Somerset, England.

*

His enthusiasms include steam locomotives and drinking real ale in proper English pubs. When not restoring his ancient house, he can be found reading political biography, chopping down trees, pointing walls, taking his much-loved Old English sheepdog for walks; and, in season, plucking pheasants. His mission in life is to provide amusement and give inspiration to others.

For

Pat Richardson

*

Birthday Honours Impression 2020

OVERTURE

An event occurred in the summer of 2004 which went almost unnoticed; we owe a debt to John Edwards for writing about it. Edwards was Tommy Steele's Touring Manager in the early days and he handled the press. He went on to become a distinguished Daily Mail journalist. The event about which Edwards was writing was the death of one John Kennedy.

This writer always felt that John Kennedy might not have been a very nice man, one who drove his discovery too hard. Mitchell notes that Steele began to clash with his managers,[1] and Kennedy certainly disliked the star's future wife. Mitchell sees him as entrepreneurial, even mercenary[2] while Everitt suggested that he and Parnes diligently 'squeezed every available penny out of the Steele market'[3] – well they would wouldn't they. But Kennedy's importance is not recognized sufficiently: and it should be. Through his promotion of Tommy Steele, he not only changed the life of one young man (and few have the opportunity to do that: and even fewer take it when it is given to them): in the course of doing so, he changed the face of British popular music for ever. As Ellis wrote: 'It would be quite true to say that if Tommy Steele had not met John Kennedy, he would not have risen to the fantastic heights he has achieved'[4] for Steele was arguably the most innovative UK rock 'n' roll act of the 1950s.[5]

So, there was this night in September 1956. Old Compton Street was washed down by the scream of a loud guitar exploding through the open-door of the 2is coffee bar. John Kennedy, Heathrow freelance photographer - and curious about the noise - pushed his way off the hot, crowded pavement and squeezed himself onto a stool by the bar. That night became important. It was the one when rock 'n' roll took off in England. Kennedy had no more ear for music than had a tree. What he knew about, and he knew a lot about, was style and promotion; and a teenage kid the punters could look up to as a hero. Tommy was an ordinary bloke and he was to become Britain's first working class rock hero[6] and our first indigenous rock 'n' roll singer.

Kennedy stared first at the faces of the girls at the tables with their drinks and cigarettes. It was layer after layer of adulation. Now he turned to the lively kid banging out some Elvis number. Presley was only heard over here on record shows and jukeboxes. From the moment that he first set eyes on him, John Kennedy knew that Tommy was a natural: but he would never have dreamed that he would become one of the most versatile and accomplished artistes of his generation.[7]

"Who's the singer?" Kennedy shouted into owner Paul Lincoln's ear. Perhaps he could take this boy into showbusiness. "Do you want to go into serious show business?" Kennedy asked him when they met outside the café. Tom said he was only on leave from the sea. He had two weeks to go. If Kennedy could show him a deal in that time then sure he would like to become a star. And that is how Tommy Steele started. Within six months he was a solid gold sensation.

Kennedy did the talking. He wheeled and dealed, he snagged a record contract and found another unknown to write songs – Lionel Bart. There had never been a man like Kennedy. Before him, show business had its own Establishment. Now there was this tall, slim, handsome guy strutting around and cutting deals in the offices of people who would not take a phone call from him earlier. Mind you, it has to be said that Kennedy's slick and daring promotion was matched by Steele's ability to charm an audience.[8] Kennedy was the first of that kind of agent-cum-manager; after him they came along like rain. Steele made a £1000 a week (£25,000 a week in the money of today). Then again there were royalties. It was fabulous money. Kennedy then took a partner. He first asked Joe Napoli an American show business agent; Napoli declined. He visited Kennedy eighteen months later; he commented 'to think that I could have had a piece' of the action; noting that Kennedy 'was loaded.'[9] Kennedy invited Larry Parnes instead. He was an investor and night clubber who brought in business expertise. Now Tommy was performing at the Café de Paris: he had become an industry with movie contracts and international recording deals.

Kennedy prospered. He bought Jaguars and had suits cut in Saville Row: he had new offices in Oxford Circus and a new flat:[10] the newspapers put the rise of rock 'n' roll down to him. Tommy was out front pushing it. Kennedy was the magician in the wings. Life became a roar. He liked jewellery and the good times. So, it was out of a bed-sit into Dorothy Foxen's great and fabled drinking club next to Harrods and into a penthouse on Half Moon Street, Mayfair.

He gambled; sat there until four in the morning opposite Sammy Davis Junior in Dorothy's, betting three queens against two pairs. There was not a second of the day which was not touched by fun and glamour. Rock 'n' roll was down to him and Tommy. History has to rate the two of them as the people who brought it from America. One million cigarettes and late nights drove Kennedy to the Californian Desert in the early 1980s so that he could breathe the hot dry air and help his chest. He died there.

So; there was a lot to remember when people gathered in the chapel of Palm Springs Mortuary for his funeral. He was only 73. And Tommy Steele has long outlived him. On the street the temperature got to 110 degrees Fahrenheit. That was also like that hot night outside the 2is in Soho so long ago. The night that Kennedy had a little bit of inspiration and a youth revolution began: and it genuinely changed the culture of the whole country: and it changed it for good.

John Edwards
Daily Mail
4th August 2004

INTRODUCTION

This writer first became aware of Tommy Steele just after he started secondary school; following Tommy's emergence, as it were, from the 2is Coffee Bar in Soho. By early 1957 Tom was a national sensation: never a day passed without the press covering his latest exploits: they were all diverting. Britain had never known anything like it. Tommy went on to fame and fortune: excelling in almost everything he did. It is remiss that no one has properly or fully documented the saga: of what happened: and how it happened: and when.

This book aims to give a flavour of how and why Tommy Steele became one of the great entertainers of our age and contributed to our country's social history in many diverse ways. A full appreciation of his work has never been forthcoming. This volume seeks to remedy that omission. It concerns a man who in his own moment in time moved people: and was indeed moved by them.

In 1966 E. W. Swanton published *The World of Cricket*. In this massive tome J. J. Warr remarked that 'he supposed that if one was granted one last wish in cricket it would be the sight of Ray Lindwall opening the bowling for Australia in a Test Match from the Nursery End at Lord's.

If this writer had one last moment in theatre it would be the sight of Tommy Steele live in concert singing a *Handful of Songs*.'

Richard R. Dolphin

The West Hatch Coliseum

<u>At the time of the Great Plague; early summer 2020</u>

Famous quote

from

Tommy Steele

"Show business is really 90 percent luck and 10 percent being able to handle it when it gets offered to you."

CHAPTER ONE

DISCOVERY

Bermondsey-born Tommy Steele has been an internationally renowned popular entertainer for over six decades. Blond haired, diminutive, usually casually dressed and boasting an unmistakable cockney accent he saw himself as an early British ambassador for rock 'n' roll.[11]

Legend has it that Tommy Steele cut his teeth at sea on the *Mauretania*[1] – a great liner in the Cunard tradition.[12] Not one bit of it, he first served as a Bell-Hop on Cunard's RMS *Scythia* (of blessed memory) sailing from England to New York for the first time on 21st April 1952.[13] Built in 1921 RMS *Scythia* was Cunard's longest serving liner until that record was passed many years later by *Queen Elizabeth 2*.

After the *Scythia* he sailed from the UK, with Furness Withy Line,[14] to join the Furness Bermuda Line's *Queen of Bermuda* to sail regularly between New York and Bermuda. He joined the 'Queen' as a bellboy. While a member of the Queen's crew he learned to play the guitar from a black plate cleaner from Bermuda. Tommy recalled "We called him Cookie and he taught me the basic chords to play in 12-bar blues. Then I bought my

---

[1] Which Tommy refers to affectionately as the *Maurie*

own guitar in Haiti and practiced for the next two years."[15] He used to jam at Bermuda nightspots with local musician Hubert Smith, who remained a life-long friend.[16]

Described by New Musical Express (NME) as a quiet ordinary London lad (and he never pretended to be anything but that)[17], Tommy ended his days at sea on the Mauretania. By that time, he was an assistant steward and gymnastic instructor. Occasionally some of the one thousand plus passengers were entertained by his Norman Wisdom impressions. Having been taught to play the guitar by crew members,[18] he admitted that he had never had a formal music lesson in his life.[19] Because he travelled to and from the United States he knew the latest rock 'n' roll songs: all of a sudden his music was fashionable: he had done more and seen more than any other subsequent British singer of the genre.

He was caught smoking on the Fire Watch in the summer of 1956 and sent ashore on 7th August 1956[20] for two weeks as a punishment. It was on that enforced leave one night in September 1956 that he strolled from the Breadbasket to the Heaven and Hell Coffee Lounge at 57 Old Compton Street: next door at number 59 was the 2is coffee bar: he saw flashing lights and went in: as he had done on several occasions before.

Let us go off at a tangent. There were a number of coffee bars in London at that time - which attracted idiosyncratic crowds - in which Tommy used to play. He writes of the first he saw: 'a new fad, shops with a counter and a Gaggia machine: they drew youngsters to small tables and subdued lighting.'[21] Among these new attractions was the Gyre and Gimble (sometimes known as 'the G' or the 'G's' – and now lost and almost forgotten) in John Adam Street. It was achingly hip and a patron was one Lionel Bart;[22] who was dazzled by Tommy.[23] Another haunt was the Breadbasket on Cleveland Street, down the road from the Middlesex Hospital; it attracted young nurses and was a magnet for a musical sailor.[24] One more was the Cat's Whisker where Tommy was photographed playing with Leon Bell.[25] He and his mates went to the coffee bars to play music: and hope that they could pick up girls.[26] One would imagine that they were successful.

Regarding the G's, one blogger recalls that 'you'd buy a coffee and they'd let you nod off on the table. And Tommy Steele used to come in there and twang on his guitar and sing and make an awful racket; all of us were just trying to have a quiet kip and we kept telling him to shut up and he wouldn't.'[27] The Vipers knew Tom from those two cafés. One of the Vipers recalls that Tommy used to go down to Brighton with them and busk on the beach: he said that he was very good in front of a crowd.[28] They used to catch the 4.40 a.m. milk train (remember the milk trains?) to the coast and perform as the *Brighton Buskers*. Once in 1956 they took £7 in forty minutes.[29] Frame suggests that Tommy was often berated for his contemporary taste and for his cocky, cockney flamboyance; but the girls were always flocking around him.

While all this was going on, Tommy Hicks had established remarkable friendships with Lionel Bart (as he became known and who he had met at the G's) and

Michael Pratt. It was the regular habit of some of the mates from the G's, when perambulating home from singing in coffee shops, to call at the Yellow Door located on a bombsite near Waterloo Station on Baylis Road opposite the Old Vic. Behind the door a commune was located.[2] Mike Pratt was the moving spirit at the place.[30] Frame notes that among a myriad of dwellers or visitors were Maurice Agis,[3] Kenneth Haigh, film star Shirley Eaton: and a young communist called Lionel Bart.[31]

Now while onboard the Mauretania, Tommy Hicks had made the acquaintance of shipmate Ivan Berg (a cousin of Bart).[32] They were both invited to a party behind the Yellow Door in February 1956. Together they found a huge bonfire, a crowd of people and in the middle a small man with a large hooked nose:[33] "That's my cousin" Berg said proudly to Hicks, "He's a printer in the East End"[34] – he was not to remain so much longer. They might have seen each other before but it was the first formal meeting between Hicks and Bart. They would never have guessed the heights to which that meeting would lead them both.

Bart was rather taken with Hicks: they formed a band called the Cavemen. So, it came about that at one of the all-night parties at the Yellow Door they wrote *Rock with the Caveman*. Yet again the rest was history. *Cavemen* was a spoof on the Piltdown Man hoax.[4] When

---

[2] Or squat: when communes did not exist
[3] Later an acclaimed sculptor
[4] A paleoanthropological fraud in which bone fragments were presented as the fossilised remains of a previously unknown early human.

they took it to a publisher he commented "It's a very interesting song – how much do you want for it?" Lionel Bart replied, "Twenty quid."

Meanwhile, Tommy Hicks (as 'Chick Hicks') had garnered experience as lead vocalist with Jack Fallon and his Sons of the Saddle in a servicemen's club at an American Air base in Ruislip; with whom he sang country music (he was introduced to the audience as one coming from the Grand Ole Opry[5]): he was paid a fiver for the gig. He often speaks of those experiences in 1954-55. As he said, those nights were "Wonderful, I was on a platform; bathed in lights, singing songs I loved and getting paid for it." In the opinion of this writer, that is one definition of happiness. He met Fallon - who was on the lookout for a guitarist - in Archer Street where, each Monday morning, musicians touted their wares in the hope of being picked by agents who were on the lookout for talent.[35] Tommy was by now semi-professional (albeit not making mega bucks) so the notion that he was discovered in the 2is and paid money for the first time is incorrect. As we shall see, the story was - and became – rather more complex than that.[36]

The 2is coffee shop – 59 Old Compton Street – was opened in 1955 by Freddie and Sammy Iranii (hence the name the 2is): originally with a third brother (so it could have been the 3is.). The brothers moved on to open a nightclub and when they did so the coffee shop was taken over by Paul Lincoln and Ray Hunter: two Australian wrestlers. Bart and Pratt managed to get

---

[5] Weekly country music stage show in Nashville

themselves hired to paint the café:[6] they painted large Cleopatra eyes on the walls of the basement[37] but they left thinners out of the paint and so customers kept turning up with dry cleaning bills.[38] On the 14th July 1956[39] the Vipers[7] (Wally Whyton among them) began performing in the 2is on a small stage in the basement. In his magisterial account of the early days of rock 'n' roll, Pete Frame relates that the proprietor was very taken with the Vipers' music and told them that he would be happy to have them come back and sing there any time. The entire British rock scene was built upon that one chance visit.[40] Quite inadvertently, they became a minor part of history. Formed in 1956 and disbanded in 1958 the Vipers were among the most successful of the early skiffle groups. They are remembered fondly by many aficionados of their style of music.

Before John Kennedy's first sighting of Tommy Hicks, Roy Tuvey (who jointly ran Trio Recording Service) had seen Tommy singing and had been minded to sign him. With this in mind he brought in Geoff Wright who was a Charing Cross Road agent. They came to some sort of informal arrangement with Tommy Hicks. The two had seen him at the Gyre and Gimble and there is a serious suggestion that it was *there* that he was really discovered: and by them. It is alleged that he *had* signed a contract with them but that, being under twenty-one, the contract was invalid as the law stood at the time.[41]

---

[6] They were paid two crates of beer – one for each i.
[7] 'Viper' was hipster slang for a marijuana smoker.

Frame recalls that Tuvey and Wright arranged for Tommy to play a guest spot with the Vipers at the 2is and invited John Kennedy along: that is a decision that they might have lived to regret.

Now, Kennedy had already worked with Wright[42] a story corroborated by The Staffords.[43] Geoff Wright had persuaded Parnes to help finance his play *The House of Shame*: which Kennedy had helped to publicize (and this writer suspects that it was a case of 'cometh the hour, cometh the man').[44] The result was an advertisement which ran: 'This week at City Varieties Music Hall, Geoff. Wright and Larry Parnes present ... the most daring story ever told *The House of Shame*.'[45]

We return to the 2is. While playing in the basement on 19th September 1956, the Vipers took a break. So it was that a young merchant seaman wearing a blue shirt and called Tommy Hicks strolled down to the basement, jumped onto the stage and began to sing *Blue Suede shoes*. Can you imagine the excitement? As noted, John Kennedy, a press photographer with the Daily Mirror, had been invited to the venue to check out the action. He was looking for someone that would set London's West End alight: he knew that Fleet Street editors were ready and anxious for real stories about rock 'n' roll: particularly with a novelty slant.[46]

And that night in the 2is coffee bar in Soho he found that for which he was looking: with a flash and a bang and a wallop he found it. But it was not the Vipers. He was electrified by Tommy Hicks' performance and personality. The crowd of youngsters in the 2is loved it too. After two more numbers, Tommy left the stage. Kennedy followed him into the street and told him that he believed that he could make him a star.

In one of the more famous conversations of the 1950s, humble seaman Tommy Hicks told John Kennedy that he was going back to sea fourteen days later. Thus, Kennedy had two weeks in which to achieve something: if Kennedy failed in that objective, the seaman would return to the Mauretania. Tommy is quoted as saying "I loved my life. The idea of people telling me they were going to make me a star was ludicrous really because no one could give me more than I already had"[47] and if you think about it, he was damned lucky.

Frame reports that when Kennedy suggested that he worked with Tommy Hicks, there was no mention of Tuvey or Wright. However, they were still very much on the scene at that point.[48]

Steele's subsequent overnight success made the basement of the 2is coffee shop the most famous music venue in the country (and do you know thirty years later a guide to Soho had never heard of it). It was only a small place though, and like many other Soho venues was usually very hot and sweaty. It featured a small eighteen-inch stage at one end, one microphone and some speakers attached to the wall. Amusingly joint owner Paul Lincoln commented later "I was completely indifferent to Tommy Steele: he did not impress me one way or the other."[49] Yet Tommy Steele made his café famous worldwide.

Kennedy was in earnest about the potential marketing of his young charge. He saw rock 'n' roll potentially as a big deal. He believed that *someone* had to lift the genre out of the Teddy Boy rut and give it class. Remember that one clergyman had delivered a sermon in which he said: "Rock 'n' roll is a revival of devil dancing, the same sort of thing that that is done in black magic rituals."[50] This was pretty heady stuff.

Kennedy perceived that British young people needed someone like Tommy Steele – a regular guy – with whom to fall in love: a boy next door. As a sales strategy it was sheer perfection.[51] Tommy talked and behaved just like all the other boys from Bermondsey (or Blackburn or Bootle) and neither he nor his formidable team of publicists[52] would let anyone forget it. Everitt, in a generally unkind feature about the artiste, observed that Tommy was a popular hero with whom the majority of adolescent girls could easily imagine themselves linked romantically. Very sensibly Tommy remarked that he looked upon the kids as his wages.[53] In fact, MacInnes believes that Kennedy earned his place in history by being the first to guess that English kids were longing for a native troubadour (and, moreover, that Tommy Steele could fill the bill).[54]

Meanwhile, and racing against time, Kennedy contacted George Martin at Parlophone[8] - a German-British record label: Martin famously turned him down saying that he was "No more than a coffee bar yodeller." Kennedy turned next to Decca (who were not so myopic)[55] whose Artists and Repertoire (A&R) manager Hugh Mendl saw him perform at the 2is and liked him. Hugh

---

[8] Sometimes referred to as 'EMI' – they owned the label

Rees Christopher Mendl was, his son noted, "To Decca what George Martin was to EMI." Mendl attended the 2is coffee bar on 23rd September and heard Tommy sing - accompanied by the Vipers – and famously said "Bring him to Decca for a sound test tomorrow." An interesting man, Steele described Hugh Mendl as being the double of Ian Bevan, who was to become his agent. He said that he "Dressed like him and spoke like him; and, in addition, chain smoked with the ash dropping perpetually onto his waistcoat."

Some years later, Hugh Mendl made a famous recording for the BBC in which he related the saga of what happened next. Tom turned up with Kennedy at Broadhurst Gardens on 24th September[56] and found that Decca had forgotten to book a studio for a test. So, it was carried out in an artistes' washroom. But all went well. A coloured bass player with the wonderful name of Major "Mule" Holly, an American then based in England, was one of the accompanists. *Rock with The Caveman* was the successful result. It was, without question, the first British rock 'n' roll record that made any impact;[57] although some claim that the song has been harshly judged by posterity. Kennedy was smart enough to have a photographer from Melody Maker on hand and the picture appeared on its front page that week.[58] Hugh Mendl and Tommy Steele were inseparable until Tom's move to Columbia seven years later: and this writer suspects that they developed great respect for each other.

Caveman was backed with *Rock Around the Town*; the latter written by Hicks himself. *Caveman* was co-written by Steele (as he was shortly to become), Lionel

Bart and Mike Pratt.⁹ He agreed a royalty of 1ᵈ a record – which was upped to 3ᵈ a disc within two years.⁵⁹

Tommy recalled the session. He remembered that Ronnie Scott said that it was the first and only time that he been asked to play a 14-bar solo. Tommy said that he had added two bars, which you do not really do, but that Scott "played them for me and it worked out fine." Tom remembered that "My family was there and they applauded after the first take." Mendl asked them to go outside "Because one can hear every clap."⁶⁰

Released on the 12th October, the record was launched on Tommy's last night at the Stork Club, the 15th October, on Jack Payne's *Off the Record*. Broadcast on a Thursday this was a programme on which Jack Payne introduced stars and personalities from showbusiness with the latest news from the record industry. Tom was paid twelve guineas for his appearance.⁶¹ He was invited back onto the programme for 24th December along with Lonnie Donegan – which may have been the famous occasion when Tommy threw a bucket of water at Donegan and viewers were left wide eyed.⁶²

Tommy related that on *Off the Record* he was "Treated like I was a burglar." The programme was run by Jack Payne: a very stiff, unamusing, stern man who was way above rock 'n' roll. Tommy said "I got an introduction in which he said: "Here's rock and roll, and you can take it or leave it"⁶³ – however within two years Payne was quoted as saying: "Steele has proved that he is

---

⁹ Future TV actor

an entertainer rather than a single stylist."[64] Steve Race[10] (who should have known better) was equally rude. Writing in Melody Maker in 1957 he opined that Tommy's music was a 'nine-day wonder; and we may already be four days through it:'[65] well, we all make mistakes. People were being scornful about rock 'n' roll. NME described Jackie Wilson's splendid rendition of *Reet Petite* as 'a strange collection of noises ranging from that of gargling to an outboard motor.'[66] At this time many people in the UK music industry slammed rock; in 1957 NME asked 'is rock 'n' roll on the way out.'[67] Well, with the benefit of hindsight, the answer was 'no ~ it was actually on the way in.'

On *Off the Record,* Tommy appeared alongside Alma Cogan (with whom, until her premature death, he was to have a long association: not least playing poker;[68] at which he was regarded as a past master) and Lonnie Donegan. The BBC had built a realistic setting - a cave - in front of which he was to sing. Kennedy reports that he received a record fifteen hundred fan letters in the week afterwards. Holt says it was 'thousands'[69] (but, as she was not around at the time, her total might be wrong).

Interestingly, although records were an important cash generator both for Decca and for the star: his management never looked upon Tommy as a recording artiste.[70] Frame reports that NME was not impressed by *Caveman*, saying it lacked the essential authentic flavour: adding that 'the best thing is Ronnie Scott's driving tenor sax.'[71] The NME changed their tune later. *Caveman*,

---

[10] A composer, pianist and radio presenter

having sold 25,000 copies in three weeks, was Number 13 in the Hit Parade within a month – it remained in the Top 20 for four weeks. By common consent, it was the first British rock 'n' roll record to enter the UK Top 20. Kennedy went to see Jimmy Phillips, General Manager at Peter Maurice, and arranged for them to publish both sides of the record. Kennedy reports that Steele, Bart and Pratt took 50% of the royalties.

Bert Weedon[11] was one of the early session men on Tommy's records. He recalled that Tommy said "Hello Bert, this is what I want you to do." Weedon played the chords back to him properly and Tommy said "Yeah that's what I meant." Weedon replied "You are a bit saucy aren't you" and Tommy began to laugh. Afterwards Weedon showed him how to play a C7 chord[12] correctly. Thirty years later they met at a Buckingham Palace event. Weedon remarked to Tommy that he had not seen him for twenty years. Tom replied "I think that I have got that C7 off alright now." They both had a good laugh about it.[72]

Tommy Hicks, having meanwhile been told that he needed a stronger name for the stage, chose "Steel" which derived from a Scandinavian grandparent (Stil). Frame reckons that the 'e' was added to Steel in error by a Decca employee.[73] We shall never know; but it stuck. Kennedy was responsible for this: not Parnes as suggested by many people – he was not yet on the scene. So renamed, Tommy Steele was to be backed by the

---

[11] A famous English guitarist and session man who died in 2012
[12] A C7 chord is similar to a regular C major chord in terms of notes: it has the same three - C, E, and G - but the C7 chord has one extra note: B♭

Steelmen; a band featuring some fine jazzmen (including saxophone player Ronnie Scott). It is fashionable today to debunk the Steelmen: jobbing musicians who were engaged to support Tommy Steele. Legend has it that they were sophisticated jazz musicians who dumbed down their craft to support an early rock 'n' roller. Maybe that is true; but goodness me they must have had a ball - not least at the famous party at the Adelphi Hotel on Ranelagh St, Liverpool after which everyone was asked to leave and Tommy was banned from the hotel. Mike and Bernie Winters had invited most of a local hospital's nursing staff - together with a sprinkling of doctors - to a party in Tom's room. Among other things they put a drunk John Kennedy to bed in someone else's room.[74] As a teenager, Tommy was, in fact, very well known as a practical joker. Anyhow, aided by Lionel Bart: Andrew Ray was apparently the butt of many of their jokes.[75] It is said that at the George Hotel[13] in Edinburgh he once switched around all the shoes left outside customers' bedrooms for cleaning[14] and altered all the times on the early morning tea list. While in Cardiff with Freddie Bell he put itching powder in the chorus girls' scanty costumes (one wonders how on earth he got at them).[76] These tricks may have gone down a bomb with some people: and, perhaps not with others. They certainly helped to give the Steele entourage a bad name which was blown up by the press at the time.

The fact is that the Steelmen backed Tommy Steele in one shape or form for two years until late 1958

---

[13] Now the InterContinental
[14] That's what they used to do.

and they played a seminal role in the early days of Britain's most influential teenage idol. Their importance needs to be recognized as such.

First was Alan Stuart on tenor sax. Alan admits that he did not rate the music too highly. Dennis Price was the pianist and was born in Birmingham. Appearing as one of the Steelmen took him to fame and some fortune. Later Price performed with the Polka Dots; they were a regular on *Sunday Night at the London Palladium*. Lastly, Leo Pollini was the drummer. No one seems to know anything about what happened to the drummer.

On 23rd October Tommy spent one day filming for the forthcoming movie *Kill Me Tomorrow*[15] in which he had a cameo role as a coffee bar singer[77] performing *Rebel Rock*.[78] Writing in the Radio Times sixty years later David Parkinson commented that 'Terence Fisher directs with little enthusiasm, but it is worth hanging in there to catch the film debut of Tommy Steele.' There is a suggestion that the success of this small part led to the offer of his first film role.

We now come to the entrance of Laurence Maurice Parnes. He and Kennedy had form. As noted, in 1954, Parnes had invested in a touring play, *The House of Shame*: the name was apposite. This became notorious after its publicist, the same John Kennedy, persuaded two actresses to stand outside the theatre during the interval dressed as prostitutes. They were arrested; but after the national press picked up the story the play took off and eventually broke even. Kennedy had a way with stunts of

---

[15] A low budget gangster film

that sort: and Fleet Street lapped them up: some of them were really rather good. The programme notes for Tom's appearance at Leicester in 1957 reveal that Hollywood companies were after Tommy; night club appearances in New York and Las Vegas were forthcoming: none of it happened. However, McAleer suggests that Tommy was not keen on going to the US as he guessed what the Americans' reaction would be to a British rocker and he did not want to go there and "Die a million deaths."[79] Dick Tatham of Record Mirror was convinced that stunts or no the public would not be fooled for very long.[80]

So, it came to pass that Parnes bumped into John Kennedy in The Sabrina,[16] a coffee bar in Soho which was underneath the Condor Club. Kennedy tapped him on the shoulder. He asked Parnes what he thought of rock 'n' roll. Parnes admitted with some embarrassment that he had never heard the term: an extraordinary admission.[81] Convinced of Tommy's potential as an entertainer - he was the wildest thing imaginable in those days[82] - Kennedy asked Parnes to come on board as joint-manager: he felt that he and his star would benefit from Parnes' business acumen.

Accordingly, he persuaded Parnes to go to see Tommy Hicks perform in the Stork Room the following week: something that was to change the face of popular music for a long while. Interestingly, Parnes had seen Tommy Hicks perform in the G's three months before. Parnes said: "I watched him – they were a tough audience,

---

[16] Named after Sabrina, then a popular and big chested starlet: ironically known to Parnes who preferred men

but they loved him – he brought the place to life with his charisma and great personality."[83]

Kennedy introduced Parnes to Steele. Tommy looked at him intently and remarked to Kennedy "He's got honest eyes:"[84] it might have been a misjudgement. So, after the performance Tommy Hicks asked Kennedy and Parnes to become his managers and a contract was signed on 26th September 1956. As he was under age the contract was signed by his parents: thus, creating the first legally binding agreement that anyone made with the future star. This is important because whatever informal agreements Tommy had made earlier with other parties they were not binding in law.

Under the agreement with Kennedy and Parnes, Tommy took 60% of gross takings. It made him: but he was lucky, later stars managed by Larry Parnes did not fare so well: that is another story. Kennedy and Parnes became a formidable (and that is the right word: you would not have wanted to tangle with them: and some did) team of publicists.[85] Parnes in particular was probably not a very nice man: he was once described as something of a loner: but it was impossible not to be fascinated by him (as he himself was fascinated sexually by young men (but not Steele)) and his aura of success.[86]

Frame relates that shortly after this, Tommy Steele bumped into another guitarist and said "I have four managers now"[87] which rather suggests that, in his own mind, Tuvey and Wright were somehow still in the frame (while in reality they were well and truly out of it). What actually happened remains a mystery. Frame relates that in 1960 a story appeared in the press headed *The Real Steele Story* written by Fraser White which was published in the *Weekly Sporting Review and Show Business*. Kennedy and Parnes brought a libel action against the writer and the paper. White suggested that he had been threatened with violence if the article was published. The article hinted that Tuvey and Wright had been carved up. The case was heard by Mr Justice Havers.[17] The evidence suggested that Tuvey and Wright were out to exploit Steele. After six days they both offered a full apology and retraction: thus, ended the involvement of the two alleged managers before Kennedy and Parnes came on the scene.[88] But there remains an underlying suspicion that Larry Parnes had not been entirely straight with Tuvey and Wright: who were probably amateurish. If so, it was just the first of many shenanigans in the history of rock 'n' roll. There is more than a suspicion that, as Sandbrook suggests,[89] Steele was a manufactured artiste who was closely controlled by his wily and audacious managers. The first suspicion is false: the second transparently true.

The Stork Room (otherwise known as the Stork Club) was a nightclub in Swallow Street north of Piccadilly and was run by 'Nightclub King' Al Burnett. In his memoire[90] Kennedy recalls that he arranged for Tommy to have an audition with Al Burnett and that he offered Tommy £20 a week for a fortnight: starting immediately. Tommy arrived on foot carrying his guitar:[91] no taxi for him. His appearance there was a great success. He was supposed to play four numbers but ended up

---

[17] Who had sentenced Ruth Ellis to death in 1955

playing thirteen.[92] Burnett was delighted and booked him for a further two weeks at 25% more pay.

The follow up record to *Cavemen* was *Doomsday Rock*. The BBC banned it. Something about the lyrics offended Auntie: this may be the reason that it failed to reach the hit parade: so perhaps the BBC effectively killed it.

Next stop; enter the great Harold Fielding. Kennedy recalls that he was talking to a retired detective in a coffee shop. The cop suggested to him that he speak with Amy Rosser who was secretary to an impresario. Fielding had become a producer of summer shows and tours for musical stars (starring among others a young Julie Andrews). Further, he had managed Sir Thomas Beecham and the Royal Philharmonic Orchestra and introduced a series of Sunday concerts at the Opera House in Blackpool. He sent his colleague Ian Bevan to see Tommy at the Stork Club. Bevan liked him. Fielding offered him a contract at £150 a week. Fielding now came up with the original idea of staging a six-week variety tour with Britain's first rock 'n' roll sensation topping the bill.

In 1956 there was no Royal Variety Show. 5th November was the time of the Suez crisis and the Queen did not think she should attend. During the day the show was called off. However, the day became notable for something else. Tommy Steele stepped onto a variety stage for the very first time - at the Sunderland Empire. Tommy writes that "To this day I get a lump in my throat when I remember the nineteen-year-old kid walking through his first stage door."[93] A year later he was himself chosen to appear at the Royal Variety Performance.[94] The tour then went on to Nottingham (12th), Sheffield (19th), Brighton Hippodrome (26th), Finsbury Park (3rd December) and Birmingham Hippodrome (10th). In the programme he was billed as Decca's new recording 'Send-sation.' By the time the tour reached Brighton the posters fairly screamed 'Rock with Decca's Dynamic Tommy Steele.' It was robust stuff: and the stunts were paying off.

So, it came to pass that Tommy Hicks made his national debut as Tommy Steele at the Sunderland Empire Theatre twice nightly at 6.15 p.m. and 8.30 p.m. The most expensive seats were 4/-. On the bill with him were (among others) Reg Thompson (Unknown to millions), Johnny Laycock (renowned for his ability to play four trumpets at once)[95] Mike and Bernie Winters (who went on to become good chums of Tommy: they had helped him to apply makeup before his first stage appearance)[96] and Thunderclap Jones (Fearsome Welsh boogie-woogie piano showman). Ian Bevan, his agent, gave him a copy of his history of the London Palladium (which years later Tom was to make his second home) inscribed 'To Tommy Steele who today joins the 'Top of the Bill' company.'[97]

Interviewed twenty years later, Tommy remembered the cobbled back street beside the stage door and the Greasy Spoon Café across the road; where he and the Steelmen spent half the first morning talking about what they would try and do that night. He also recalled a fireman who 'presented himself on stage' and remembered how he was told he needed to have a fire bucket beside him through the performance.[98] Tommy remembered firemen standing in the wings because there were fears that his electric guitar might explode.[99]

Charles Govey, writing in NME, described him as a rip-roaring bundle of energy and rhythm and North East journalist J. Cummings reported 'squeals, moans, whoops and yells' greeting his first performance at the Empire. Cummings referred to 'this nineteen-year-old youth' combining 'boyish shyness with simple vibrant ability.' He wrote that Tommy was 'gifted with a catchy exuberance.'[100] Eighteen days later Tommy had been voted 8th outstanding British Male Singer in NME's annual polls. 'He can please the old as well as send the young' reported the Sunderland Echo[101] which was clearly quite switched on itself. The Stage noted 'how the crowd enjoyed his closing rock 'n' roll numbers' and commented on the pleasing way in which he presented his act.[102]

One paper described it thus: 'At the theatre, things went differently. The screamers were in action as the curtain rose and the thin, leggy lad with the freshly shampooed hair growing out of his head like a clump of grass mercilessly worked up the frenzy and the rhythmical, brain-washing thunder of the claps for twenty minutes or so. There was only one short pause. This was to introduce the members of his 'Combo.' He explained that if this was not done nicely, they would duck him after the show. (Indignant cries of "Ooh, yer," and "Don't be cruel.") In a very short time, he has developed an alarmingly powerful stage technique, for all his blinking at the spotlights and there was more than a hint of arrogance in the way in which he abruptly left his frantic admirers with only one short curtain call; to the sobering mercies of the squarest of national anthems.'[103]

Tommy has related a number of times how after the show in his first week he returned with the other members of the cast to their digs and over coffee and sandwiches heard their stories of life on the road as variety stars. He was mesmerized and decided there and then that he wanted to learn all that he could about stagecraft. He checked out of his hotel in Nottingham in the second week and moved into digs with the rest of the cast.[104] He must have felt more comfortable with them.

As noted, the variety show moved on to London to St Thomas Road where then stood one of the city's most famous variety halls and theatres: the Finsbury Park Empire. It was Moss Empire's main theatre outside the West End. Tom reached there on 8th December. Kennedy recalls that many people turned up without tickets and stood in the foyer – refusing to move – in the hopes of hearing the performance. It was Tommy's first London triumph ~ the first of many. On the other hand, there was a sour note: one reviewer commented 'It seemed little short of a miracle that this nineteen-year-old youth could receive such a rapturous oration (sic) for the little musical talent he displayed.'[105]

Keith Goodwin reported for NME that he had seen Tommy and thought that he would be packing them in for a long time to come. A couple of hundred fans tried to break down the stage door on the first night. It was reported that Tommy played excellent rhythm guitar: which is interesting in itself as many people questioned his ability with the instrument including Dick Hall who said it would be kinder not to mention his playing.[106] There were reports of teenage girls screaming, fainting and generally getting hysterical on a scale never seen before.

Interestingly the question of *screaming* which started big time with the Steele concerts was to resonate down the years. December 1963 saw the Performing Right Tribunal interrogating Harold Fielding over his responsibility for the growth of the phenomenon: which was equalled but not surpassed later at Beatles concerts. Fielding accepted responsibility and said that he regretted having started the practice. Fielding, Parnes and others were contesting the rates of payment being sought by the Performing Right Society.[107]

Kennedy describes it as a 'happy tour.' But he talks of the constant demands on the police as teenage girls tried to break the stage door down. It was while they were playing Sheffield that Tommy formed his own football team made up of young artistes and they played games against local schools. There is one famous photograph of Tommy autographing a girl's back:[108] he would not be allowed to do it today. Those were simpler and happier times.

Kennedy recalled that while Tommy was appearing at Brighton, he was asked to appear at a private cabaret at Claridge's Hotel. This he did to great acclaim from the guests. As a result of which, he received an invitation from Major Donald Neville-Willing, an elfin little man with a monocle,[109] the effete entertainment manager at the Café de Paris,[110] to follow Marlene Dietrich's season at the Café.

At Christmas, the Kent Messenger reported that a prankster switched on *Rock with the Cavemen* instead of *Good King Wenceslas* during the Christmas procession through Ashford.[111] Unlike John Lennon, Tommy Steele never claimed to be more popular than Jesus: but by now he *was* a household name.[112]

1957 was to be the year when skiffle and Tommy Steele dominated the hit parade[113] and the year in which his career as a rocker reached its pinnacle.[114] 11th January will be remembered as long as Tom lives for it was on that day that his version of *Singing the Blues* reached Number One in the Hit Parade. It was there for one week only. In spite of a long and distinguished career he was never to repeat *that* triumph. *Singing the Blues* was first recorded in the US by Marty Robbins and then famously covered by Guy Mitchell: it was *his* hit and Tommy covered it.[115] A distinctive feature of the record was the whistling. Tommy is always amused to tell the story that the whistling was performed by Mike Sammes – who whistled through Bronco lavatory paper to give it the required effect – because he himself cannot whistle. There was – and remains – much discussion among pseudo intellectuals about his rendition. A number of critics took umbrage at the voice he adopted. Surely the truth is that he was a young man trying to adopt an American voice for what was after all an America song. Whatever, his version had a fresher treatment and sounded more like rock 'n' roll. The record was issued on 1st December 1956 and was publicized by Decca as 'the greatest sensation yet by the sensationally successful' star. They knew what they were talking about.

However, it was on 21st January in the historic Café de Paris on Coventry Street - London's home of international cabaret, a Mecca of the upper class - that Tommy Steele established his name in fashionable circles. "That caf," as Tommy's mother scornfully called it, was then one of London smartest niteries in an age when the aristocracy still counted for something.[116]

Kennedy recalls that a late cancellation resulted in Tommy being offered a two-week contract at £200 a week. Against the expectation of many he was a triumph ~ one witnessed by most leading newspapers. It was reported that dressed in a shiny blue outfit Tom took the stage with the remarkable Dennis Price on piano 'attacking the notes with intriguing abandon and vigour.' One celebrity that he met there was Cynthia Oberholzer the South African Beauty Queen: and Hartnell model.[117] He overcame a bad start when every fuse in the Café blew as he went on stage: he just walked around the tables singing to the diners while the electrics were fixed. He received wonderful reviews the next day. Noël Coward, with his rapid clipped upper-class diction and who proved to be an unlikely devotee,[118] saw him and told him that 'the theatre was calling him:' he went to see him every night.[119]

27th January, Tommy appeared on *Sunday Night at the London Palladium* for the first time;[120] hosted by Tommy Trinder he sang *Knee Deep in the Blues*.[121] He was asked to extend his engagement at the Café for a further two weeks. It was impossible because this contract was to be followed with another long series of gigs that started with a one-night stand on Sunday 3rd February at the de Montford Hall, Leicester. He appeared in a famous photograph with a group of three adoring young women all wearing 'Tommy' sweaters. Trevor Philpott wrote in *Picture Post* 'It's ninety per cent youthful exuberance. There is not a trace of sex, real or implied. The Steelmen all writhe around the stage; even the pianist has no stool. They freely admit that none of the antics have anything to do with music. As Tommy would put it "We do it for laughs."'[122]

Philpott drew attention to an important point recognized by few at the time. Never before – never before – had young people enjoyed the opportunity of doing 'teenage things' in a teenage manner; but it was, he commented, 'like killing-day at some fantastic piggery.' It was new, it was a revelation, it was a release and Tommy Steele changed their lives. Tom 'slayed them' alright. Diane, Judy and Pat from 212 Wigston Lane wrote to the Leicester Mercury 'We think he is the mostest. The way he digs rock 'n' roll sends us all screaming with delight.'[123] Wonderful. Ellis noted that when 'Tommy Steele came on, I saw this boy absolutely tear the audience apart, the excitement in the theatre was unbelievable.'[124] Here there was no sign of the expected moral outrage and he wore a special sweater – a Rhythm Pullover - made in Leicester.[125] The programme for his Leicester performances advises that 'The Tommy Steele Shoe' could be bought locally at Hiltons.

He proceeded to Chiswick (4th) and went on to Peterborough (11th) and the Newcastle Empire (18th).It was while appearing at the Chiswick Empire (timely as it was demolished two and a half years later) that Lionel Bart introduced Tommy to his future wife Ann Donoughue.[18] Ann, from Leeds, was a dancer at the Windmill where her stage name was Ann Donati. After the show she invited him to a party on the other side of London. They travelled in discomfort in Tommy's getaway housepainter's van. Tommy remembers that they were surrounded by paint tins and turpentine while people banged on the roof.[126] By the time they reached their destination the party was over; so, Tom took her for coffee at the Sabrina coffee bar.[127] It was love at first sight; the rest is history. He told Nunn that "There were no other girls in my life: I love her so much it's a thing you can't talk about."[128]

The BBC had decided that there was a market for a programme aimed at a younger audience. Until that time, the BBC had a closed period of television between 6.00 p.m. and 7.00 p.m. which was referred to as the 'Toddlers' Truce.'[129] Th truce ended on 16th February and it never came back: *The Six-Five Special* (of blessed memory) was the result. Today *Six-Five Special* would be regarded as old hat: at the time it was a revolution: and an hour devoted to teenagers: and it would not have happened without Tommy Steele. He starred for the first time on Saturday 2nd March[130] and the next four episodes.

The Six-Five Special was probably one of the most famous programmes ever produced for a largely teenage

---

[18] That is how Tommy spells her name in his book: and *he* should know: he often refers to her as 'Annie'

audience. It was built initially around the personality of Tommy Steele who was paid one hundred and fifty guineas[19] for appearing. It is reported that Larry Parnes wanted five hundred guineas which, he claimed, he could have extracted from ITV.[131] Tommy himself remembers it as a mixed bag of music and fun. Jack Good[20] had this idea of not giving the audience seats and letting them roam around the studio. Jack said: "Let them roam about and if they come into shot, so be it." Some people were surprised that Good got away with it, especially as he was so young. Everyone wondered what he knew about television: the answer is probably very little. Tommy remembered someone in the audience who looked like Bill Haley. Jack said, "It's not Bill Haley, it's a lookalike. We will pick him up in the audience shots and people will think that Bill Haley comes to our show."[132] Tommy was on television again on the 24th February for ATV in bandleader Jack Jackson's Show.[21]

Then came the *Tommy Steele Story*. Anglo-Amalgamated Films were thinking of making a film about rock 'n' roll. Music publisher Jimmy Phillips introduced John Kennedy to Nat Cohen and Stuart Levy (the colourful owners of Anglo-Amalgamated)[133] with a view to making a film: Tommy later remarked that there was a

---

[19] A guinea was one pound and one shilling = £1.05: as it was 5% more than £1 it was a fashionable form of payment in business contracts
[20] A short-haired, bespectacled Oxford graduate: he created the fast-paced Six-Five Special for the BBC
[21] *The Jack Jackson Show* was broadcast on a Saturday evening. It came from the Embassy Club in Bond Street and was a mixture of interviews with stars, music and showbusiness news.

touch of madness about them both. Having agreed to make the film, they were persuaded to make its focus the life of Tommy Steele. The story was told modestly: from the lessons in hospital while he was recovering from a strained back, and life in the Merchant Navy, to the recording studios and the Café de Paris. Between episodes there was the parlour in the terraced house in Frean Street and Mum and Dad; and through it all the young hero remained cheerfully surprised at the fuss and the size of the cheques. All this was too amiable and innocent to cause riots; and there was breathing space between songs.[134] The posters boasted 'The TRUE story of Britain's most sensational entertainer.'[135] Not bad for four of five months of stardom. Lionel Bart said "Here's this guy, he's only twenty, he ain't even started his own story. I suggested they should not be all rock 'n' roll songs: let's have some cockney songs and let's have some calypso."[136] Picturegoer was mildly generous, it said 'it is a modest little biopic with a simplicity well within the scope of his limited acting ability.'[137] Well, there you have it.

Never before had a film been made about a star's life just months after he was discovered. It was to be filmed at Beaconsfield in studios built in 1921 by George Clark Productions. There was a rush of production activity some years later and among new start-ups was The British Lion Film Corporation Ltd. Producer Peter Rogers took over Beaconsfield Films Ltd in 1956. Production of the film was underway on 24th February. It was shot in less than three weeks and was in cinemas in May. Tommy was photographed at the film studios with his new Ford Zephyr number TLN139: his new girlfriend visited the studios every day. Tommy wrote the songs together with Mike Pratt and Lionel Bart (both twenty-five): they completed the task in seven days. Later in 1957, both gave up their jobs in order to write the songs for Tom's second film. Steele himself was paid £3,000 for the lead role in the film about the first twenty years of his life. Charles Govey, NME reporter, visited him on set while making the film. He reported that Tom was staying in a flat nearby. He said that after leaving the studios in the evening he went into Uxbridge to visit the cinema. and on the way back he purchased fish and chips and chucked the paper over a hedge.

Secretly previewed at the Savoy Cinema Luton,[22] the film premièred in the UK at the Rialto Cinema, Coventry Street, on 30th May (with general release on Monday 24th June) and in the US at the Paramount Brooklyn (where Alan Freed's[23] rock 'n' roll shows played). The Paramount was a former movie palace at 1 University Plaza and there the film launched as *Rock Around the World*. It went on to be one of the few British films screened in Russia. A clip from the film was shown on BBC *Picture Parade*[24] on Monday 17th June.[138]

Douglas Adams was the manager of the old ABC Cinema in Kirkaldy. He was out to promote the *Tommy Steele Story*. His daring ploy drew a great deal of press attention. He obtained a life-size cardboard cut-out of

---

[22] Later the Cannon cinema it closed in 2000
[23] US disc jockey who popularized the term rock 'n' roll (once slang for sexual intercourse)
[24] A weekly magazine programme of films and film personalities introduced by Peter Haigh.

Tommy Steele. It was initially displayed in the cinema foyer; however, it disappeared one day only to be discovered in the harbour. Naturally the papers obliged with headlines like; *Tommy Steele found floating in Kirkcaldy Harbour.*'[139]

NME reported that a slow rock number - *Butterfingers* - was expected to be the big hit from the movie. So, it proved to be: and it remains so sixty years afterwards: and Tom sang it in his pantomime at Liverpool that Christmas. An NME reviewer of *Handful of Songs / Water, Water* opined that this record could be very important in establishing Tommy as a long-time recording star: he was a far-sighted man.

It was during this period that Tom agreed to close the bill in a charity concert to be staged on 17th February at the London Coliseum for the Sportsman's Aid Society. It was an event never forgotten by the star or by his management. The show overran badly. Customers started to leave to catch the last bus home. Quite intolerably the organizers tried to bring the curtain down on the star in mid-performance. There was nearly a riot: no one present ever forgot or forgave.

Kennedy and Parnes sent Tommy, his mother and brother Colin for a holiday in Majorca because he was about to start a gruelling tour with a major American star. On his return, he appeared at the Odeon Guildford on Sunday 17th March at 5.15 p.m. and 8.00 p.m. Presented by John Smith he was supported by the Mick Mulligan Band with George Melly and Desmond Lane. In the 1950s George Melly and the Mulligan Band became synonymous with a jazz lifestyle that involved imbibing copious amounts of alcohol and frenetic and varied sexual activity at all hours of the day and night. Inevitably the Band's performances were quite often affected. By then, however, the Band's brand of revivalist 'trad' jazz was going out of fashion. They recognized this when they did this concert with Tommy Steele. George Melly recalled later, "We did our set and the audience was quieter than usual. Then Tommy Steele came on and these small girls exploded into shrieks." MacInnes too wrote of 'kids shrieking, moaning, stomping, swooning and crying out in ecstasy.'[140] Melly's trombonist, **Frank Parr** - who was famously depressive - said "We would all be on the breadline."[141] Interestingly when Tommy wanted to appear in Portsmouth on the Sabbath[25] he was not allowed to do so: and the city fathers in Swansea thought Lonnie Donegan 'unsuitable.'[142]

Tuesday 16th April, Tommy appeared at the Royal Albert Hall in one of the BBC's Third Annual *Festival of Dance Music* the compere was Rikki Fulton with whom Tom was to work in Liverpool eight months later. This was followed by his appearance at the Edinburgh Empire (April 1st) and the Empire Leeds (8th). On 22nd April on the BBC Home Service, Tommy was the guest on *Desert Island Discs* for the first time.[143] He included the Two Bills from Bermondsey with their rendition of *What a Mouth*. Saturday 4th May Tommy appeared on ABC's *Saturday Spectacular* with Jack Buchannan; with whom he sang a duet.

---

[25] **Sunday**: a day of religious observance and abstinence from work: rigorously observed in the '50s

The *Tommy Steele Story* was launched just in time to herald his second major British tour (announced in Melody Maker on 30th March) - for which he was allegedly paid £1000 a week[144] - on which he was billed jointly with the crack American outfit Freddie Bell and the Bellboys. Getting Bell to the UK was complicated, as exchange deals had to be agreed with the Musicians' Union. Bell and his Bellboys finally arrived in May: it was to be the first (of many later) rock 'n' roll package to tour the UK.[145]

Bell headlined the tour that featured Britain's first home-grown rock star. It opened at the Liverpool Empire (6.20 p.m. and 8.35 p.m.): Reg Thompson was there again as were Mike and Bernie Winters. The programme notes that Tommy's rise had 'left everyone gasping.' It proceeded to the Cardiff Gaumont (13th), The Dominion Tottenham Court Road (20th) where (1) it was noted that Tommy wore rock 'n' roll shoes made by E. K. Coles Ltd of Burton Latimer[146] and (2) he made his London theatre stage debut wearing said shoes. It proceeded to the Glasgow Empire (27th) where Doug Heath saw him in action. Heath wrote "You did not want to be part of Freddie Bell and the Bellboys: they were never going to win. The lassies doon[26] the front were into their Mantra[27] "Tommy, Tommy, Tommy." They were hand-jiving; some were in tears: all of them were screaming. Then Tommy came on bathed in pale blue light, clad in an electric blue cowboy shirt with a guitar as big as him. It was a cold night. I left the Empire with a warm glow."[147]

---

[26] 'down'
[27] A mantra is a sacred utterance

It sounds like Doug Heath and the lassies doon the front had a wonderful time.

We believe that Bill Kenwright's[28] admiration for the entertainer was kindled when Tommy, the Steelmen and Freddie Bell were playing the Liverpool Empire. The stars were staying at the Adelphi. The local papers carried headlines 'Steele thrown out of hotel.' This followed, Kennedy reported, a riotous party in Tommy's suite. There were a hundred revellers eating Steele food and drinking Steele booze: Freddie Bell, John Kennedy and Tommy Steele started to throw them out. Apparently when they reached Cardiff the local hoteliers anticipated an orgy. So well-known had Tommy become – sometimes favourably, sometimes not – that by this time there was hardly a person in Britain who did not know his name. This writer seems to remember a poll conducted in the late 1950s in which Tommy was found to the most famous person in Britain (notwithstanding the Queen). However, many people simply tried to ignore rock 'n' roll: not least the Prime Minister[29] - as did every one of his class.[148]

By the end of the run, Steele rather than Bell was closing the show, but the two singers became close friends.[149] On 14th June, NME reported Freddie Bell saying that it was four weeks full of fun; and that he found Tommy unconscious of his stardom. In fact, Freddie and Tommy formed a warm, jokey friendship.[150] In Cardiff, Tom locked Freddie outside their hotel on a

---

[28] British theatre producer, Chairman of Everton FC and later friend of Tommy Steele
[29] Harold Macmillan

fire escape: but Bell got his own back. Bell loved Tom's cockney ("Let's have a butchers").[30] Tom received a tremendous teenage reception when they reached the Tottenham Court Road Dominion where 2895 people turned up twice nightly. Wearing an immaculate white shirt and shoelace tie it was said that Tommy received a welcome equalling any that Johnnie Ray[31] ever received. It is interesting to note that Harold Fielding subsequently told NME that he regarded the John Barry Seven as Britain's answer to the Bellboys. Proof of his admiration for them was that he signed them up to appear with Tommy in a series of matinee shows during the following summer to be staged at the Blackpool Palace theatre: it was their first full-time public engagement.[151] Billeted at the sedate Majestic Hotel, in St Annes on Sea,[32] Tommy was asked to leave after playing the drums in the ballroom at 3 a.m.[152]

Tommy now began another variety tour taking him first to the Bristol Hippodrome (June 3rd). At the Manchester Palace (10th) 'the screamers were in action as the curtain rose, and the thin, leggy lad with the freshly shampooed hair growing out of his head like a clump of grass mercilessly worked up the frenzy and the rhythmical brain-washing thunder of claps.'[153] He went on to Hanley Theatre Royal (17th), the Birmingham Hippodrome (24th) ('You'll feel fitter on Atkinsons Bitter'[33] boasted the programme), Aberdeen Capitol (1st July) (where he

---

[30] To "have a butcher's" - means to have a look – Cockney rhyming slang
[31] Flamboyant, almost deaf, bisexual singer
[32] No longer majestic – it was demolished 1975
[33] Aston Park Brewery – later taken over by Mitchells and Butler

sparked public hysteria),[154] Stockton Globe (8th), Coventry (15th), Morecombe (22nd) and The Garrick Theatre Southport (29th).[34] On Friday 9th August, NME reported that Tommy had attracted more customers to the Stockton Globe than any British or American artiste before him: breaking every existing box office record for the theatre. Fourteen policemen were called to hold the crowds back as 31,000 people saw him perform during the week. This was all heady stuff.

He proceeded to the Gloucester Regal[35] (19th August). Sheila Petrie recalls that while Tommy was playing there, he passed his driving test at the first attempt. The local paper reported that he 'rocked the examiner Mr George Hepworth' – in the light of his subsequent speeding fines, Mr Hepworth might have wished later that he had been more stringent. Tommy then proceeded to Cheltenham to buy a red and grey Citroen. Petrie also recalls that one of the dancers was Tom's future wife. She remembers that there so many girls outside the stage door on the last night that the staff turned hosepipes on them. She also remembers that Tommy staged a show at Gloucester gaol: the first time that he had played in a prison. While playing the Regal, two women collapsed in the audience and were carried out[155] (it probably happened all the time).

Meanwhile as noted earlier, Tommy was appearing at Blackpool's Palace Theatre for a four-week season of *The Tommy Steele Afternoon Show* running

---

[34] 'In Person Britain's Teenage Idol'
[35] Now Wetherspoon's Regal

from 22nd July until 17th August, Mondays to Saturdays he appeared daily at 2.30 p.m. Also, on the programme along with the John Barry Seven was the ubiquitous Reg Thompson and the Ken-Tones[36] (all this while appearing at Morecombe and Southport in the evenings). In 1992, Pat Richardson was talking to Les Want of the Ken-Tones. He told her that Tom used to disappear to spend time with his girlfriend and it was his job to bring him back to the theatre.[156] On the 14th July Tommy appeared in Associated Television's *Sunday Night at Blackpool*: and reprised the show on the 18th August.

20th July 1957 was a historic day for the UK record industry. The Long-Playing record (LP) from the *Tommy Steele Story* became the first LP by a British artiste to top UK albums' chart: it stayed there for four weeks.[157] The Staffords suggest that for students of popular culture it is unmissable.[158]

Then on Sunday 18th August Tommy made his debut as a compère on ATV's *Meet the Stars*: by now he had become Britain's top box office attraction. While appearing at Blackpool he had to be smuggled out of his theatre using decoy cars. Success breeds success. Kennedy reports that it was impossible for Tommy to appear anywhere in public without being mobbed and assaulted physically.

By now Betty Pargiter (fondly remembered by older fans) had become Secretary to the Tommy Steele Fan Club (which then had over 10,000 members):[159] helped by two assistant secretaries. They were based at

---

[36] An English vocal group

Suite 21, 53 Haymarket: and it cost 5/- a year[37] to join. One fan, Margaret McLean, wrote Tommy a ten-page letter every day. Poor chap. His agent put all this popularity down to "Heaps of natural talent" and noted that he smoked sixty cigarettes a week and did not drink alcohol (he said that the strongest drug he ever took was two aspirins).[160] It was said that his greatest talent was that he came across as an ordinary likeable British kid.[161]

On 8th August[162] the Hicks family moved from Frean Street in Bermondsey to a house in Ravensbourne Park, Catford named *Shiralee* after Tommy's own composition for the Peter Finch[38] film of the same name. The new house was fitted with contemporary telephones coloured white – because when he was a sailor, Tommy always dreamed of having white telephones.[163] What a very simple ambition. The move was reported and shown in British cinemas on Pathé News[164] and there are a multitude of photographs of this national event to be seen online.[165] There was a housewarming party there on 1st September.[166] Many years later their old Frean Street home was demolished and new flats built on the site: which is today appropriately named *Hicks House*.

So, this extraordinary year rolled on. Around this time, it was rumoured wildly that Tommy had a heart condition. The story was started by the Sunday Pictorial (which clearly had a heart condition of its own as it no longer exists as such; having become the Sunday Mirror in 1963). The reality was that he had been called up for

---

[37] 25p
[38] Famous English-Australian actor

National Service[39] and had been excused because he had fallen arches:[40] ironically the same fate befell Marty Wilde in April 1959:[167] one has to wonder why rockers were afflicted so singularly. Tommy's exemption was nothing to do with his time in the merchant navy for five years - as some people suggest.[168] So he was spared the various experiences of Elvis Presley and Terry Dene.

Less than twelve months after leaving the sea – and now a star of stage and screen – Tommy began a love affair with Scandinavia. Anglo-Amalgamated asked his management to send Tommy to Scandinavia to promote the *Tommy Steele Story*: evidentially the promotion was successful; the film beat every available record including *Gone with the Wind*. He was in Copenhagen, Stockholm, Oslo and Brussels from 5th to 13th September.[169] When he appeared at the Anglais Cinema in Stockholm on 9th September a local newspaper reported that 'Six radio cars and two dozen Östermalm police officers were called out to keep the fans in order' and, in addition, the cinema was damaged. Kennedy described the applause there as 'Like thunder.'[170] In Copenhagen, Tom was greeted by Customs' official Birgit Sommer; she asked him if he had anything to declare. Safely through customs, 15,000 fans had gathered and persuaded Tommy to give an impromptu concert. In Copenhagen he thanked his audience in broken Danish (which he had learned from a phrase book) for turning up: they were bowled over.[171]

---

[39] A government programme of compulsory military service – usually two years: UK call-ups ended in December 1960
[40] Flat feet, or 'fallen arches', are where your feet press flat on the ground.

Tommy proceeded to Oslo: where his guitar was damaged by mobs of fans. He returned to the UK to replace the damaged instrument from where he went on to Brussels. A famous photograph was taken there of armed police guarding the edge of the stage. So, it came about that Tommy Steele was described as 'the first youth star in Europe;' and he was the first star marketed through merchandising. As noted, there were shoes: in addition, there were trousers, shirts, jackets and blouses for sale; all adorned with Tommy Steele's image[172] not forgetting brooches, guitars, bracelets earrings and rock 'n' roll suits.[173]

An unattributed newspaper, which we think was the Daily Mail, reported that Tom visited a Nice hotel with Ann Donoghue, who was referred to as his 'secretary'. He was sick to death with all the reporters trying to make something out of his genuine love for the girl who was to become his wife.[174]

One writer referred to the 'hold' that Tommy had gained on Danish teenagers after only one performance (at the Tivoli Concert Hall).[175] An academic paper reports that the first big foreign name associated with rock 'n' roll, Tommy Steele, was first presented in Denmark as the British counterpart to Elvis Presley - only in a much more acceptable form - with Steele himself being widely presented by Danish media as a nice, down to earth homely British boy whose rock 'n' roll performance was considered more theatrical than real.[176] This suggestion is borne out by a British writer who noted that Tommy's greatest talent was that he was an ordinary likeable British kid who obviously got a kick out of life.[177]

During his next promotional tour of Denmark, there was a competition for girls to enter in which they were to say why they would like to be Tommy Steele's companion: the prize was to be a day with the star. Emphasis was placed on the fact that the idol was an ordinary boy and not a dangerous, sexy beast like Elvis Presley. Aarhus parents could relax at the thought of their daughter spending time with someone like Tommy Steele.[178] It was won by a girl named Hanne who took the star around Tivoli Gardens one evening. They went bicycling and shopping together. A year later he visited her and talked to her doctor father about pain in his guitar arm.[179] Then Tommy was back on the road at the Chatham Ritz (16th September) and the Hull Regal (23rd). He appeared on *Sunday Night at the London Palladium* on 29th September and performed *Hey You*.[180] After which he spent two weeks on holiday in Cornwall ~ which must have been sorely needed ~ and he would have been made welcome in a part of England to which he had been evacuated during the war.[41]

On 31st August, Melody Maker announced that Saturday 19th October (the nearest Saturday to Tommy's first television appearance in 1956) would be a truly momentous day. The BBC would mark the most extraordinary, sensational first year in show business history ever recorded with its production of *The Golden Year*. This was what dear Tony Hancock would have called 'Six-inch banner headline stuff.'

---

[41] Tommy Steele was evacuated to Roskear

The show opened with the Vernon Girls ushering Tommy down a golden staircase to the melodious sound of his rendition of *A Handful of Songs*. Twenty-two years later he talked of how a stage hand, Alf, sat with him at the top of the stairs waiting for the show to begin. Alf, thinking that Tommy was nervous, offered him a Woodbine.[42] Mike and Bernie Winters participated; they had opened with him at Sunderland eleven months before and the three had become good friends. Jack Good had gone to see Tommy in concert and instead had signed up the brothers for Six-Five Special: it was the break that made the Winters household names: so, they had much for which to be grateful to him. Gilbert Harding participated and claimed to be "enraptured and entranced." One has to ask oneself why this grumpy old critic felt like that. Ruby Murray took part: and the whole show was put together by Ernest Maxin. An unidentified dancer had to learn Tommy's routine for the show and then teach it to him. She commented that he picked up the routine from her at 'an amazing rate.' She wrote that she 'saluted his ability to learn and memorize' with such speed. He was always a very bright man.

While Tommy was appearing with Freddie Bell at the London Dominion, and aroused by the success of the *Tommy Steele Story*, Anglo Amalgamated approached Kennedy and Parnes about a second film. Ever the shrewd fixer, Parnes negotiated a deal worth five times the money Tommy was paid for the first film. Four hundred people applied to play Tommy's 'double' in the film: a role for which NME had been soliciting applicants.

---

[42] A very strong brand of untipped cigarettes

While all this was going on, Tommy received a call while staying in his parents' new home in Catford. It was from Ken Park in South Africa. The ensuing conversation resulted in an extraordinary experience; a two-week tour of South Africa to take place after he had played *Goldilocks* over Christmas at the Royal Court Theatre in Liverpool. The Melody Maker trumpeted that Tommy was to embark upon a world tour in 1958: starting in South Africa, moving on to Australia and then America. After Africa, he never reached the rest of the world on that journey.[181]

The film was to be a take on Mark Twain's 1881 novel *The Prince and the Pauper*.[182] The idea came from Tommy himself who had enjoyed the story since he was a kid.[183] Filming began on 21st October with a tentative release date of Easter 1958. Kennedy tells the famous story of how Tom was accommodated in a luxury caravan which he persuaded the film company to give to him when the filming was completed. While filming was going on Lionel Bart asked Tommy to appear in a musical that he was writing tentatively called *Petticoat Lane*.[184] Tommy was not really enthused. The idea eventually morphed into *Oliver:* perhaps his enthusiasm should not have been under control.

November was the beginning of a month of pure gold for Tommy Steele. First this unprecedented tribute. Next an invitation to appear at the Royal Command Film Performance at the Odeon Leicester Square on the 4th November. This gala event is hosted each year by the Cinema and Television Benevolent Fund: at which it features a major film première. Attended by members of the royal family, it raises money for charity. In 1957 the nominated film was MGM's *Les Girls* and starred Gene Kelly (with whom Tommy was to make a television show eight years later). It was the last film that Gene Kelly made for MGM. Kennedy reports that the Queen told Tommy that 'her daughter was already a fan.'

The run of gold continued. Tommy was invited to appear at the 29th Royal Variety Performance[43] at the London Palladium on 18th November. Although Mario Lanza was top of the bill - and Tommy was billed underneath Judy Garland and Frankie Vaughan[44] - he was invited to close the bill: there was a big row about that from older, jealous performers. Interestingly, the poster for the Performance billed him as "Skiffle with Tommy Steele": Tom always said that "He could take skiffle or leave it."

Kennedy recalls that Tommy ran onto the stage to muted applause. He invited the very starchy audience to clap their hands to his beat. They largely declined. Tommy has retold many times how the Queen Mother leant on the edge of the Royal Box and joined in. He always reckoned that she saved his bacon: that is an illustration of what you call 'knowing how to behave.' As Tommy wrote: 'for the first time in its history the house rocked and I lived to roll another day.'[185] In closing the bill, Kennedy reminds us the entire cast joined Tommy on stage strumming guitars. The Daily Sketch praised his performance and nominated him as their *Boy of the Year*:[186]

---

[43] A Royal Command Performance
[44] But above Gracie Fields and Vera Lynn!

which may or may not have aroused him. Members of the starchy audience referred to were critical of almost everything that he did; but, as Mitchell noted, he had begun to impress even the most sceptical of critics.[187]

CHAPTER TWO

FIRST STEPS TO STARDOM

So, we turn to his triumph over Christmas 1957. Tommy Steele's links with the great city of Liverpool go back to the days when he sailed from the Mersey as a cabin boy on board Cunard ships. Harold Fielding determined to produce *Goldilocks and the Three Bears*[45] at the Royal Court Theatre commencing on the 24th December: starring the 'Fabulous and sensational' Tommy Steele. It was his first experience of a 'book show'.

Tommy received his first lessons in dancing from choreographer Malcolm Goddard while rehearsing for *Goldilocks*.[188] Tommy himself remarked that "It was the first show I ever did where I could act and dance and it was the turning point of my career."[189] The pantomime was described by one critic as a 'gay and lively production and abounding in everything a good pantomime should have:' one in which Tommy proved that he was a showman to his fingertips.

It proved to be a production of which Director Freddie Carpenter could be proud. He had been born in Melbourne and was a hugely successful theatre director for many years. In rehearsals for *Goldilocks and the Three*

---

[45] Most expensive seats 42/-

Bears, Carpenter said to him "You will not need your guitar." The book was by David Croft: with the additional help of Rikki Fulton he ensured a performance of sterling merit. One unidentified reviewer noted that Tommy had answered as effectively as possible all those (and there were many in the chattering classes) who could not envisualize him in a pantomime.

Now his career in entertainment really took off. While appearing in the show he met - and was hugely influenced by - the great pantomime dame Rikki Fulton. Ann Howard who appeared with him described him as a 'nice man.'[190]

Tommy recalls that during an episode of *Goldilocks*, the local paper reported him telling the audience to "Shut your gobs" when he wanted teenage girls to stop screaming. His mother was quite taken by girls chasing him and screaming at him: she said "Oh Tommy. Oh Love."[191] It was during his time in *Goldilocks* that he fell in love with showbusiness.

And then there was that matinee on 19th February 1958. Local students got hold of the pantomime script: they destroyed all the gags: it was all part of a Rag Week[46] stunt. It was enough to turn any respectable rock singer off higher education students for life. He brought the curtain down and cancelled the performance. Every time he visits Liverpool someone reminds him of the incident. It was, said Tom, an "Unforgivable act of hooliganism." He wrote to the University of Liverpool Guild of Students

---

[46] An annual event in which university students do strange things to raise money for charity

saying "If this is the sort of thing that they learn at university, then thank God I did not go to university."[192]

Kennedy recalled that there was a scene in *Goldilocks* where the comic had to hurl a custard pie at Tommy. He would duck and let someone else take the hit. He moved around the stage each night so that someone unsuspecting got hit. The entire theatre staff was in the auditorium each day to watch the joke. Kennedy goes on to tell a favourite story. Tom saw an urchin on the street in Liverpool. He was dirty without shoes and sitting in the gutter splashing his feet. Tom took him by the hand to his hotel and gave him tea. He gave him £5 and arranged for him to call at the theatre next day to collect a ticket for every night of the show's run. In the aftermath of Jimmy Saville, you could not do it today.

Richardson recalls a delightful story from the time. Tommy was leaving the theatre on opening night at 10.20 p.m. A man was passing clutching his turkey and a Christmas tree: as one does. The crowd surged forward towards the star, knocking the turkey and tree from the man's hands. He started fighting the crowd; as one would. Two policemen were called and arrested the thirty-four-year-old man who was drunk. He was given an absolute discharge.[193]

Columnist Malcolm Johns commented that by 1958 Tommy Steele had become accepted: and had become rather more important than a passing boy-wonder. This was a perceptive observation. Many of the stuffed middle classes initially wrote him off as a one-night wonder: they were all proved wrong. NME columnist

George Harrison noted, after *Goldilocks*, that 'Tommy is a sensational discovery for pantomime.' He wrote that he 'moved with the ease of a veteran.' One commentator remarked 'Tommy Steele is a sensation in this medium. He has a confident easy-going style and works tremendously hard. This pantomime establishes young Steele as an all-round entertainer of tremendous ability.'[194] Even as early as 1957, the star was seeking an approach and an audience which was as wide and as catholic as possible with a view to cultivating a more satisfying career.[195] So great was the success of the production that he presented highlights on *Sunday Night at the London Palladium* on the 5th January 1958 presented by Robert Morley:[47] Steele allegedly received nearly £1000 for his fifteen-minute appearance.[196]

Amusingly Tommy told Spencer Leigh about the accommodation provided for him while he was appearing in the pantomime. He was billeted in a caravan in a field in Ormskirk (off the East Lancs Road)[48] and went there every night. It was right in the middle of a field. You cannot really imagine Tommy Steele as a 'field person.' He said: "I must have been out of my mind. There was no electricity and no water, but I managed it. I had my bath and my showers at the theatre and I used the caravan for eating and sleeping. It was a wonderful idea but it was freezing cold. It was January. But, no one found me and it was really blissful. I could not stay anywhere in Liverpool because the fans would be outside the hotels and clambering up the drainpipes. You look at the Adelphi

---

[47] The recording of this episode is missing
[48] It links Liverpool to Salford

and imagine someone trying to climb up there; but that is what happened. I could not get digs as I would be discovered and I was in a quandary. I had to get my sleep: I had two shows a day and it was a very hard routine." He said to his management "You can drive me to the caravan." Fans would not follow in cars as they would be too young and anyway hardly anyone had cars at that time."[197]

22nd February witnessed a special *Six Five Special birthday edition.* Tommy called the programme live: and the BBC showed a clip from the *Tommy Steele Story.*[198]

At the conclusion of *Goldilocks,* Tommy and the Steelmen sailed on the 27th February for South Africa aboard Union-Castle Line's RMMV[49] *Winchester Castle.* It is believed that Parnes released a story that Tommy did not wish to fly because of the very recent Munich Air Disaster.[199] It is thought that this was the reason that Parnes was roundly condemned by NME. Be that as it may, the Steele entourage arrived by sea in Cape Town on the 13th March. While they were away the Ivor Novello Awards for 1957 were presented. The Most Outstanding Song of the Year Musically and Lyrically was Tommy's masterpiece *A Handful of Songs* written jointly by Lionel Bart, Michael Pratt **and** Tommy Steele. Due to his absence his mother Betty Hicks collected his award which was a bronze statuette.[200] This writer imagines that she did this with very considerable grace. *The Tommy Steele Story* actually generated three Novello Awards the others being Best Novelty Song[50] and Best Film Score.[201]

---

[49] Royal Mail Motor Vessel

So, they arrived in Africa. The opening concert in Cape Town was scheduled for 15th March. Later appearances were planned[202] for Port Elizabeth (?), Pretoria (banned), Durban (?) (where they had tea with the Lord Mayor), Johannesburg (24th/26th), Salisbury (?) and Bulawayo (27th). He was the first international rock 'n' roll singer to tour South Africa: another first for this global trendsetter. So great was the fear of rioting in Johannesburg that the city council made the promoter take out special insurance in case the City Hall was damaged by fans.

The tour turned out to be the stuff of legends. The guy who made the bookings was not in show business and was no businessman. The Steele contingent sailed without having receiving promised advanced payments. They arrived in Cape Town to be greeted by uncontrolled mobs of Ducktails[51] some of whom they feared were out to kill Tommy. Local radio had been announcing his imminent arrival for twenty-four hours. Tommy and his managers ended up taking refuge in the Rotunda hotel at Camps Bay four miles out of town.

There was very strong feeling against Steele and his music from the right-wing white intelligentsia (they may not have been as intelligent as they thought themselves). Both the man and his music were regarded as symbols of depravity. The Dutch Reformed Church and the Afrikaans cultural organisations prevailed upon Pretoria City Council to ban his appearance there. Tommy

---

[50] *Water, Water*
[51] The African equivalent of Teddy Boys

responded "If I am good enough to appear before the Queen of England surely, I am good enough to appear before Pretoria City Council." Touché Mr Steele,[52] apparently, he was not.[203] The Cape Times reported that its Mayor had cancelled a reception for the star[204]/[205] whilst at the same time its reporter applauded 'his real cool rhythm.' One paper commented that 'Half the secret of his performance is that you want to mother him: the other is his real cool music: **and that smile**'[206] (it was described as a 'million dollar smile').[207] Interestingly, writing four years later, MacInnes suggested that 'as long as a million Mums enfold his image to their indulgent bosoms this overnight star is in show business for keeps:'[208] sixty years afterwards how prescient his comments proved to be.

Mitchell comments that his homeliness proved incredibly winning.[209] It is interesting to pause here: the actuality is that, as Mitchell points out, the image that he projected to audiences in all parts of the world was unfailingly lively, and youthfully exuberant but of a man who was decisively non-threating and boyishly non-sexual.[210] In a spoof in one African concert (when he appeared in Sea Port, Cape Town) he was dubbed 'Sir Tommy' during his performance.[211] Sixty two years later the real honour still awaits.

Concerts were segregated and Tommy insisted that for every white concert he would put on one for a black audience: they did not argue about it: and he personally drew attention to apartheid. In spite of what

---

[52] As Oscar Hammerstein II once remarked to him.

some of the ignorant toffs thought in the UK: this was no ordinary young man. He commented that some of the white shows were boycotted because he was doing the black ones; they thought he was decadent. In Cape Town there was a protest. The first twelve rows of the first performance were full of doctors, schoolteachers and professional men, all in suits with red carnations with their arms folded. It went on for an hour[212] "They were stone faced" he said.[213]

The atmosphere was charged with enthusiasm wherever Tommy played *and* he performed to peaceful audiences who enjoyed his music. When Tommy Steele played to a non-white audience at the Bantu Men's Social Centre[53] in central Johannesburg[214] he received rave reviews. The Johannesburg programme described him as 'Britain's wonder boy of entertainment.' However, some reviews were starchy: 'He is not a good singer and he does not know how to play a guitar' reported New Age on 3rd April.[215]

His ability as a guitarist was challenged by several people (including Bert Weedon). It is reported that someone made the acid remark "As an actor Tommy Steele is a very good guitar player (and he's not that hot at that either)."[216] On the other hand some people write quite well of his abilities[217] and it is reported that before he was discovered he was considered to be a proficient guitar player and had backed bluesman Josh White on one of his early trips to the U.K.[218]

---

[53] **Founded** by the Rev'd Ray E. Phillips of the American Board Mission

During Tommy's tour, twenty-five boys and girls were arrested in Springs[54] for having a rock 'n' roll session in the basement of a building: although no charges were made. A few days after this incident, the British rock singer Terry Dene[55] was deemed an 'undesirable person' by the South African Department of Home Affairs: accordingly, he was prohibited from touring the country.[219] The Steele contingent sailed back to UK on 31st March en route to a visit to Scandinavia to be followed by a UK variety tour scheduled to last for six months. They must have been glad to get home. For the record, if you will excuse the pun, while he was in South Africa his record *Nairobi* was released: it was written by Bob Merrill who wrote *Sugar* on which Tommy's doomed 1991 production of *Some Like it Hot* was based.[220]

So, the spring of 1958 saw Tommy back for seven days in his beloved Denmark. Travelling to the airport to fly there, his car was involved in a slight accident and he missed his plane. Tommy was determined to let no one down. He chartered a private aircraft and arrived in time for his first show.[221] He went to Copenhagen (14th, 15th,16th), Aarhus (17th), Aalborg (26th) and Odense's Fyens Forum (27th). April 17th saw a 21-year-old Englishman with a cream-colored guitar around his neck on stage in Aarhus Hall in front of 3,500 delirious young people. It was the first of two sell-out concerts that evening for the first real European teen idol.

The Aarhus Social Democratic newspaper was on the spot. Its first and last pages on the 18th April carried

---

[54] A formerly independent town in the east of Ekurhuleni in the Gauteng province 30 miles from Johannesburg
[55] An undistinguished British rock music singer popular in the late 1950s who was briefly famous in his time and place

the headline[56] '7000 very young Aarhusians commended their very last night, so the roof of the Aarhus Hall was about to rise.' The reporter continued 'Thursday afternoon Tommy Steele landed at Aarhus Airport; thus, commenced his conquest of Jutland. The happy and smiling Tommy Steele immediately took to Aarhus. He was strictly guarded by his permanent bodyguard - the Steelmen. In addition to being Tommy's own orchestra, in their spare time all four men have to take care of Tommy. The curtains separated and revealed the hero, Tommy, on stage wearing blue jeans and embroidered trousers; a fringed white dress shirt and a cream-colored guitar on a string around his neck. Tommy sang, played and danced. He lay down on his back on the stage floor and behaved so silly that children went wild with excitement. Lisa Rich uses the same formulation when she remembers the big night: 'I remember when he sang *A Handful of Songs* and shook his head, then seethed throughout the hall; people were wild with enthusiasm.' 27th April, he performed in Odense:[57] there are a number of photographs taken of him in the city available to see online.[222]

While he was away the *Duke Wore Jeans* was premièred. There was a pre-release run at the Dominion Theatre Tottenham Court Road beginning on 23rd March. The film went on general release on 30th March. It was screened in the British West Indies on 7th April.[223] His fans heard eight new Steele, Bart, Pratt songs: and witnessed his first screen kiss. Frame recalls that co-star June Laverick said: "The director did not say 'cut' so we held the kiss for ages until we both got the giggles."[224]

---

[56] Translated as written
[57] birthplace of Hans Christian Andersen

Wednesday the 9th April he appeared on AR's *Cool for Cats* presented by Kent Walton: both *Princess* and the evocative *Happy Guitar* were featured from the film. Then came the Caird Hall incident.

Tom was scheduled to tour nationally from April to November: starting at Dundee. It was a disaster. Tommy related the bare bones of the story to Spencer Leigh[225] many years later. Roughly what happened was that he was playing this one-night stand at the Caird Hall on 30th April. Rock 'n' roll had really taken off nationwide: everywhere he went it was a really big event. There were always as many people outside the theatre as inside: they all wanted to get in. It was a precursor of the fame to hit the Beatles years later. He *really* was famous now: to such an extent that he was mentioned in *Thunderball*[226] and in the *Wild Man of the Woods* edition of *Hancock's Half Hour* broadcast on 22nd January 1957 the star announced that he was taking a copy of *Rock Around* (sic) *the Caveman* with him to the woods on his becoming a recluse![227]

Anyhow, in Dundee Tommy was waiting to go on stage and the manager of the theatre told him that, so great was the demand for tickets, they had sold the seats reserved for a choir or symphony orchestra. This meant people sitting on the stage behind the performers. Tom started his act and suddenly felt a tug on his arm. There was a little girl offering a sweet. He said "Thank you very much" and gave her a little kiss.

She returned to her seat behind him on the stage along with three hundred and ninety-nine other people.

There were no security staff. All had been going well until then. However, this little red-headed girl had given Tommy a sweet and got a kiss; so now a couple of hundred other kids behind him thought that they would do the same. They came off their seats and down through the organ gallery past the Steelmen smashing through the drums and the amplifiers. At which point the audience in the front began to rush forward too. The artiste was stuck in the middle and was unable to escape. He was almost torn apart. They ripped his shirt off. He fainted. His left arm was scratched and bruised, leaving him unable to use it; hair was pulled from his head. The crowd was held back and Tommy was pulled unconscious to the door leading backstage. He collapsed in the passage with his guitar still hanging around his neck. A doctor and an ambulance were sent for. One steward remarked, "I have never experienced anything like that. I thought he was going to be killed." Steele vowed then he would never play Dundee again – and he never has done.[228]

The orthopaedic specialist at Edinburgh Royal Infirmary said that he needed deep massage but they could not do anything until the cuts had subsided. The tour was cancelled as Tommy could not play his guitar. He travelled to Ireland to try to recover from the ordeal and meanwhile DISC[58] reported that there was a general air of mystery about the whole situation.[229]

Kennedy claimed that the tour was in the hands of a big cinema chain: they had contracts with Harold Fielding: he in turn had contracts with Kennedy and

---

[58] DISC was a weekly pop newspaper published from 1958 to 1975

Parnes. Tommy was sued by Kennedy and Parnes as well as by Harold Fielding. They all claimed that Tommy could go on stage without a guitar. They lost. Tommy was seen by a Harley Street specialist[59] who confirmed that he was in no state to perform.

The judge said: "This boy is being handed around like a silver chalice."[230] Tommy was forced to take two months off work. He said afterwards: "It made a great impression on me 'cause for a while I had to go and see a psychiatrist about it."[231] This writer believes that by that time the novelty of thousands of girls hurling themselves at him must well and truly have worn off.

25th May saw the publication in hardback of *Tommy Steele* by John Kennedy. It was the first rock biography.[60] A paperback edition appeared a year later with updated photographs and text: it is compulsive reading.

6th June 1958 saw the announcement of Tommy's engagement to Ann Donoghue who was at the time appearing in *Expresso Bongo*. The betrothal was a controversial concern to his managers (particularly John Kennedy). The story was announced in California (of all places): 'thousands of teen-age British girls today mourned the loss of their idol, tousle-haired rock 'n' roll star Tommy Steele. They lost him to love. On Wednesday he announced his engagement to showgirl Ann Donoghue.' Said Steele: "I don't want to hurt my fans; but love is love."[232]

---

[59] Dr Stafford Clark, Guy's Hospital
[60] And a whole stream followed later

Tommy made his comeback on 16th June at Coventry: so, his six-month tour resumed. Later, came the news that he was going to feature as an exhibit at Madame Tussauds'[61] - for which he presented a set of his own clothes. So, it came about that on 20th September, he became the first popular singer to be immortalised there in wax.[233]

This writer believes that it was on the visit to Coventry referred to above that Tommy saw the light. He left the theatre one evening after a performance and was approached by two teenage girls. One thrust a bag into his hand together with an eye brow pencil. "Sign this," she is reported as demanding. The star remonstrated with her, saying that this was not a very nice way to ask for something from him. One of them replied: "Listen you. We can make you and we can break you." It was a Road to Damascus moment[62] for him. He realized that this creature was right. He determined there and then that when his current contract ended in November he was going to finish with rock 'n' roll. Perhaps it was what you might whimsically call *Fortuosity*. His own mother, always the most sensible of people, had said to him "People are very fickle. One day you are up; next day you are down."[234] As ever, Mrs Hicks was spot on.

At 10.40 p.m. on Sundays in July and August Tommy presented a series of eight pre-recorded programmes styled *A Handful of Discs* on BBC's Light Programme: it was his debut as a disc jockey and was

---

[61] World famous waxworks museum in London;
[62] A sudden turning point in one's life: refers to the New Testament conversion of Saint Paul the Apostle

delayed from May because of his injuries. He got paid one hundred guineas a programme (and forty guineas later for an appearance on *Housewives' Choice*)[235] more than twice the weekly wage of BBC disc jockeys ten years later. In fact, the music press in general watched in amazement as Tommy progressed to ever greater heights and by 1958 one of his managers claimed that his protégé's first 'cool million' was within his grasp[236] which might have annoyed some critics who themselves lacked a million cool or otherwise - Parnes did whip up controversy. As a disc jockey, one BBC executive said, he was "Just the ticket: really natural and refreshingly un-BBC."[237] The Corporation was very stuffy in those days.

In August, immediately after appearing at the Bournemouth Winter Gardens on the 4th, the star went on a three-week holiday in southern France (where, not surprisingly, he found that he was unknown).[238] The break must have been much needed. On his return, he said that he felt much fitter. On 1st September, he recommenced his extended – and interrupted – tour at Southsea South Parade Pier.[63] The variety bill at Southsea broke every previous box office record for the theatre; the previous record being held by the great Jimmy Edwards and Billy Cotton.

Then on Monday 27th October Tommy Steele was featured on *This is Your Life*: clear evidence of his staying power. He was the seventieth celebrity featured: and, in those far off days, the programme went out live. It was the fifth programme in the fourth series: a copy still survives.

---

[63] It had been built in the time of Henry VIII

The presenter was, of course, the immortal Eamonn Andrews. Tommy was surprised, as most guests were, by Andrews as he arrived at the BBC television studios thinking that had had come to "Have a picture took for Crackerjack." A journalist recalled that, on the way to the studios, Tommy called at Alma Cogan's apartment and, afterwards, had very real difficulty getting a taxi to the studios. He almost failed to make (what he thought) was the photo shoot. His agent Ian Bevan was party to the secret and managed to hail a cab for the star at the very last minute.

The BBC put all their clocks back by ten minutes so as to ensure that Tommy would not realize the significance of his arrival time. Nor did he; for he was not wearing a watch himself. As one person who was present noted, Tom fell for the ruse and suddenly the clocks changed back to present time. The story unfolded as guests associated with his past appeared on the stage one by one. They included:

- Ernest Maxim, well-known as a television producer in the 50s who had produced *The Golden Year* for Tommy Steele on BBC. He was quoted as saying "There is much more to Tommy than a guitar-playing rock 'n' roll singer, his real talent is for writing and straight acting. He has a really wonderful mind; one full of ideas."
- Freddy Carpenter - responsible for directing *Goldilocks* and later *Cinderella*
- Herbert Smith - who produced *The Six-Five Special* and *The Tommy Steele Story*

- Chas McDevitt - who appeared in *The Tommy Steele Story* and had become famous in 1956 for *Freight Train*
- Jack Campion - who first gave Tommy an interest in playing the guitar
- Lionel Bart and Mike Pratt - co-writers of so many of Tommy's early hits and originated *Rock with the Cavemen* with him. They were paid seven guineas to appear.[239]
- Thomas Hicks, Betty Hicks, Colin and Roy and his sister, Sandra.

One writer - commenting that Tom survived the ordeal honourably - wondered where John Kennedy and Larry Parnes were: commenting also on the absence of Ann Donoghue: of whom, of course, the Steele management did not approve. Apparently, the Steele office described the programme as 'rather weird. More to the point, perhaps there was always something 'rather weird' about the relationship of the management with its star.

On 1st November Tommy made his one and only guest appearance on ABC-TV's *Oh Boy!* It was reported that during the live broadcast Tommy rocked up a storm with the Dallas Boys.[240] Cliff Richard appeared on *Oh Boy!* and was roundly condemned. NME reported thus: 'Tommy Steele became the nation's teenage idol without resorting to indecent, short sighted vulgarity.[241] Tommy refrained from using sexual suggestiveness in his physical performance.'[242] The point really was that he was such an outstanding performer that he simply had no need to resort to sexual gimmicks – as so many other singers did in later years.

Saturday 15th November saw Tommy's last appearance in a UK theatre for eighteen months (apart from two charity shows at the London Palladium). It was at the Granada Kettering[64] (of all places): one wonders how many people in Kettering still remember the occasion. Sadly, it was the last time that he ever appeared together with the Steelmen. Richardson reports that it was sixty-three minutes before he was able to leave the stage and midnight before he got away from the theatre. He had invited his teenage audience to conga around the theatre: a local police man is reported as remarking: "Do not worry: Steele has them under control."[243] It was in character: he constantly demonstrated 'a natural command of his audience.'[244] Sensible copper.

At the conclusion of what had become a second golden year, Tommy was signed to star in *Cinderella* together with Jimmy Edwards and Yana. It was to be Yana's debut both in pantomime and in the West End. It was a triumph for a lad barely twenty-two. The London Evening News reported that it was the most sumptuous and beautiful *Cinderella* that the capital had ever seen.

As noted, exactly a year before, Tommy Steele - then Britain's first teenage idol - had played *Goldilocks* at Liverpool's Royal Court Theatre. That was the first time that he had worked with Freddie Carpenter. The winning combination was such a success that impresario Harold Fielding determined to build upon it and turn the pairing

---

[64] It became a bingo hall in 1974

into a 1958 triumph: for Tommy Steele, for himself and for all the rest of the cast.

The publicity for the pantomime at the London Coliseum was enormous: it was the first pantomime to be staged there since *Humpty Dumpty* in 1944. Wherever you went on public transport in the capital you saw posters advertising what was to become a blockbuster. The original pink poster proclaimed the opening on 18th December but so great was the triumph that revised mauve posters appeared after the opening night carrying the endorsement of the London Evening News.

Before rehearsals commenced, Tommy Steele went to meet Rodgers and Hammerstein in New York. He described Hammerstein (who was dead from stomach cancer within eighteen months) as a man with enormous hands. He often speaks of Hammerstein's attempts to get him to enunciate his language better: Tommy commented at the time, he 'huddles in the front stalls at every rehearsal picking up any deviation from his lyrics.'[245] Interestingly, Hammerstein referred to Tommy as a young man 'with great charm and grace' – what a gracious thing to say. He continued 'He is obviously loved by his audience.'[246]

Interestingly, an unknown journalist interviewed Tommy in 1963 and wrote 'he sat behind a desk in his manager's office radiating an easy and utterly unselfconscious charm. He continued, 'nature has endowed him with what one can only describe as *instant likeability*.'[247]

Harold Fielding spent £100,000 (a huge amount of money in that era) bringing the show to the West End. It was the largest sum at the time ever invested in a London production and it was the first show to use the full resources of the Coliseum since *White Horse Inn*[65] in 1931.[66] Fielding assembled a team of all the talents in order to present the show. The Director was Freddie Carpenter: he was responsible for three other pantomimes running simultaneously, but this was his first in the capital. It would have brought back memories as he danced in Prince Littler's[67] *Cinderella* at the Coliseum in 1936. The designer was Loudon Sainthill, an Australian stage and costume specialist; then aged forty and at the height of his powers. His early designs were spoken of as 'sumptuous and exuberantly splendid.' Later, he was the designer for *Half a Sixpence*. Sainthill spent £12,500 alone on the ballroom scene. There were three revolving stages,[68] an orchestra of forty and a cast of seventy.[248] It would be difficult for an outsider to imagine the time and effort spent on a production of such magnitude; but Fielding writes of the army of seamstresses, carpenters and electricians engaged in the production: all with the purpose of bringing a fairy story to life.

Not all the reviews were orgasmic. Anthony Heap[69] opined: 'The rock 'n' roll idol brought to the part little but an atrocious cockney accent' while Alan Brien,[70]

---

[65] A musical comedy that was a huge success on Broadway and in London
[66] It was the first proper musical at The London Coliseum
[67] British impresario and theatre owner
[68] Three turntables one inside another
[69] A London diarist

displaying the characteristic of his class, thought Steele's timing was embarrassingly erratic and that he moved as stiffly as a stilt-dancer.'[249] In all probability, Mr Brien would have done the same. It was not the characteristic of the metropolitan elite to be generous to a bright young cockney learning the ropes. This writer guesses they were both square: the general view was that Tommy Steele 'The golden boy from Bermondsey'[71] played a wonderful Buttons. Maybe it was sufficient, as Tommy recalls, that among others "Noël Coward, Rex Harrison and Laurence Olivier all came backstage and told me that I had it."[250]

He was twenty-two years old the day before the show opened and had enjoyed what was described as 'the most sensational, most publicized and most lucrative rise to stardom ever known in showbusiness.' Buttons was regarded by many as a trivial part. Jimmy Edwards was a wonderful King and, in the finale in the Baron's drawing room, he sang a ditty written not by Rodgers and Hammerstein but by Tommy Steele himself. The song was *You and Me*. Tommy was given credit in later versions of the theatre programme: at the personal written suggestion of Oscar Hammerstein. He was a big man. Tommy injured his ankle early in April 1959 and his understudy Ted Rogers took over the part: it was *his* big breakthrough. The injury prevented Tom from appearing in BBC's Drumbeat on the 11th.

Yana[72] was born in Romford and became famous as a model and actress in the 1950s. She played Cinderella

---

[70] A journalist for *many* papers
[71] As he was described in the souvenir brochure
[72] Real name Pamela Guard

while at the height of her fame. The cast was then boosted by Kenneth Williams and Ted Durante who played the ugly sisters ~~~~ continuing a great British theatrical tradition of men playing pantomime dames. The prince was Bruce Trent. Tommy always referred to the wonderful orchestra. It was of a size that you could not see at a similar production in the UK today. Bobby Howell was the Musical Director. Tommy's favourite song was *A Very Special Day* which originally came from Rodgers and Hammerstein's *Me and Juliet*.[73] Highlights of the songs and music were broadcast on the BBC Light Programme on Christmas night.[251] It was a real seasonal treat for the nation.

---

[73] A 1953 musical: their sixth stage collaboration

CHAPTER THREE

I WANNA BE AN ALL-ROUND ENTERTAINER

Far from the least interesting thing that happened in Tommy's 'second golden year' was the painting of him by Jim Isherwood. He was a well-known Wigan artist and painted Tommy Steele with two heads – with the intention of communicating the dynamism of Britain's first teenage idol (he also produced a nude of Dusty Springfield which made her furious: well it would wouldn't it).

We should not leave 1958 without reference to an extraordinary story that broke in 2008 and which attracted widespread media attention. Tommy's then producer spoke on BBC Radio 2 about an alleged meeting in London between Tommy Steele and Elvis Presley.[252] It is alleged that Presley met Tommy in London and that Tom gave him a guided tour of the city. Tommy was quoted as saying that he swore that the story would never be divulged publicly and he regretted that it had leaked out. The story may be hokum pokum *or* it may be the real McCoy:[74] either way the truth will die with Steele. But 1958 was an even more momentous year if it *did* happen.

---

[74] No one is can be sure which is the real McCoy of all the claimed origins of this expression

1st January 1959 Tommy appeared in the *1959 Show*.²⁵³/⁷⁵ He sang *Deck of Cards* (the song which likens a deck of cards to the Holy Bible) which lead to some complaints: and two songs from his pantomime *Cinderella*.²⁵⁴ 13th February he featured *Elevator Rock* on *Cool for Cats*. Tommy was booked to appear for a second guest spot on *Oh Boy!* on the 4th April. This appearance was postponed for a week until 11th due to other prior commitments. However, on the 10th as noted above, Tommy broke his ankle in an accident and had to cancel the live performance. He was due to perform his new single *Hiawatha*:²⁵⁵ however, he did go along to the studio to speak to fans: but did not appear on the show.

Production of Tom's third film, *Tommy the Toreador,* on location in Spain was scheduled to start on 4th May running through to July. It was shot in the little Spanish town of Alcalá de Guadiara twelve miles south east of Seville⁷⁶ (where Tommy was photographed drinking from a large leather bottle)²⁵⁶ *and,* most importantly, in the simply wonderful Plaza del Toros⁷⁷ de la Real Maestranza de Caballería de Sevilla. Tommy said that walking into the bullring in the blazing sun was more of an ordeal than many of the great first nights that lay ahead of him.²⁵⁷ The film was planned as a big budget, lavish colour production: expensive enough to show that the studios were taking Tommy seriously.²⁵⁸ Tommy was paid £50,000: twice what Sir John Mills would have

---

⁷⁵ This show was later rebranded *Hippodrome*
⁷⁶ Since when Seville has grown to such an extent that Alcalá is now a suburb.
⁷⁷ Bullring

commanded.²⁵⁹ Just imagine it, Kennedy and Parnes must have been rolling in the isles - £20,000 of that was theirs.

 Co-star Janet Munro was under contract with Walt Disney but was released for this film: she had planned to have her tonsils out but postponed the operation in order to make the film. Associated British-Pathé originally planned a huge launch for 18th November where it was scheduled to open in the Warner West End cinema, Leicester Square. However, the launch was delayed. As Tom's Fan Club held their annual get together at London's Empire Rooms, Tottenham Court Road, everyone attending proceeded by coach to the Bermondsey Rialto[78] on St James' Road to watch the film. It was always said of Bermondsey that Tommy had a real feel for the place and its people. He greeted everyone inside the door. Highlights from *Toreador* were broadcast on *BBC Picture Parade* on 23rd November. It was reviewed in *She* magazine (which at the time was regarded as quite unconventional and risqué). *She* referred to the star as 'toothy Tommy Steele (talented too)' and opined that the movie was for 'the young - and young in heart:' it was a very apt review for their women readers.

 The official release of the film was re-scheduled for 21st December followed by general release four days later. *Little White Bull* was voted a 'miss' by the entire panel on *Juke Box Jury* – it went on to be a monster hit for the star and proved to be the song which completed his transition from pop singer to family entertainer. As the Staffords wrote eloquently 'like Gene Kelly singing *I got*

---

[78] Now demolished and turned into a block of flats

Rhythm to street urchins or like Danny Kay singing *The Ugly Duckling* to a little boy, Tommy settled himself down with a group of Spanish children and sang them a story that started *Once upon a time there was a little white bull.* [260] It was a moment of greatness in his career: and is remembered still and fondly by generations of admirers. Tommy donated the royalties from the record to charity and the NME reported in July 1960 that an initial £800 had gone to children's cancer research. The song is sometimes played at funerals:[261] presumably of cows.

Tommy the Toreador was the end of the road for Bart, Pratt and Bennett[79] and really the apotheosis of their relationship. Bart and Pratt wanted to do different things: and Tom was moving in other directions (star of blockbusters, author, painter, sculptor, squash champion, composer).[262] The team had written thirty songs for Tommy in just over two years.[263] It was a wonderful record and had made Bart's name: and helped to make Steele's. It is probably true to say that at the end Pratt (who was no longer pulling his weight) was aptly named.

At this time, the *Woman's Day Sheet Library No: 2* included Tommy in their feature *My Song and I* for which he nominated *Shiralee* as the song that he had written of which he was most proud "That's the best piece of song writing yours truly has done to date" he wrote. He had, of course, named his parents' new house after the song.

August saw Tommy Steele in Moscow together with Richard Todd and blond bombshell Carole Lesley.

---

[79] Bennett was a pseudonym for Tommy Steele

They were attending the first ever *Moscow Film Festival*. He was pictured on his return on the 7th wearing a (Russian) fur hat and carrying a Balalaika.[80] The Guardian reported that *The Tommy Steele Story* was shown at a cinema actually inside the Kremlin. The visit was featured on his return on BBC's *Words and Music*. On one of the three days, Steele turned up in Red Square plus guitar and gave an impromptu show that seems to have gone down quite well. Manager Kennedy started off the clapping along with a few other Brits present, photographers and the *Mirror* man. They kept it up for three hours and the audience gradually increased to three hundred. "The police did not say anything. They just blew whistles if anyone stepped off the kerb," Tom is reported as saying, "They are pretty square in Red Square. They do not understand really, you know."[264] But, they did not seem to have thought Steele or his rocking were really decadent and they liked the film. Tommy said they "Really loved it. I was quite surprised because they've banned that type of music and the film was packed with it."[265]

Interviewed by BBC News on the 5th August, he reported the existence of a black market in records – except for classical ones – and that he found Russians just like any other people albeit dressed differently: but he said that he had never received any fan mail from their countrymen (or presumably women).[266] On the 13th August there was film of him in Moscow in the BBC *Words and Music* programme.

---

[80] A Russian stringed musical instrument with a triangular wooden body

The summer saw the issue of *Give. Give. Give. / Tallahassee Lassie*; the two sides on this disc could justifiably be regarded as his last rock 'n' roll recordings. The critics considered Tommy's cover of Freddie Cannon's hit (*Lassie*) as 'perfectly credible rock 'n' roll.'[267]

During 1959 Tommy recorded a series of Saturday Spectaculars for ATV - *This Particular Show:* the first was broadcast on 19th September: another on the 14th November. For one the BBC refused Tommy permission to use David Jacobs[81] in a *Juke Box Jury* comedy sketch. The sketch went ahead in October with another BBC personality[82] taking Jacobs' part.[268] The Spectaculars featured Tommy introducing other stars, talking, dancing, singing and cracking jokes (at which he hoped that they would laugh). The last of the shows was recorded on 1st December and transmitted on Boxing Day.[269] It included the Show Biz XI and All-Star XI football teams, together with Morecambe and Wise. Tommy was a keen player for the former and spent one weekend with them in Jersey playing soccer for charity. In October, Tommy appeared in Billy Smart's Circus on Clapham Common in what was then an annual charity performance in aid of the Variety Club; Burma, the elephant, caused a stir by walking over both Jayne Mansfield[83] and Tommy.[270] On Thursday 29th highlights from this were broadcast on the BBC's *Children's Newsreel*.[84] Tommy appeared as a cowboy at the Circus.[271]

---

[81] Not the controversial lawyer. Broadcaster and Chairman of *Juke Box Jury*
[82] Announcer McDonald Hobley
[83] Glamorous American actress
[84] A very popular programme at that time

Meanwhile on 25th October, Tommy started filming again, this time at Twickenham studios. His fourth film was to be *Light up the Sky* based on Robert Storey's play *Touch it Light* (initially renamed as *Rise and Shine*). It was to be Tommy's first dramatic role. Apparently, Tommy contributed £7,500 towards the cost.[272] This was the beginning of the end of Tommy Steele as a pop singer. He was finished with being mauled to death at concerts and would bid farewell to competing in the singles charts.[273] The title song was recorded by Decca (with a strange number *Drunken Guitar* as the flip side). It may have been the last Lionel Bart track that he ever recorded. It was all set for release having been sent out to reviewers: it also featured on *Juke Box Jury* on Saturday 6th August (1960).[274] The disc was then pulled at the last minute: Larry Parnes said that *he* was responsible.

By 1960, in an article about the record industry for Cherie,[85] he admitted he had "Risen slightly above rock 'n' roll" he continued "I consider myself lucky that I have."[275] However, if his role as the UK's rock'n'roll instigator and originator has been largely airbrushed out of the history books, it clearly does not seem to have bothered him.[276] It does bother some other people. By 1960 he had become almost an establishment figure and was the subject of a debate (which is still broadcast occasionally) on BBC's *Any Questions* when a questioner asked whether the panel would like their son to grown up to emulate Field Marshal Montgomery,[86] Peter May[87] or

---

[85] #7, 12th November 1960
[86] One time Chief of the Imperial General Staff
[87] The public-school educated captain of England's cricket team

Tommy Steele. The matter aroused fierce debate with Russell Braddon[88] being particularly outspoken (against Steele) on the subject. He claimed that Steele "Murdered the Queen's English" (which, as he himself was Australian, was a bit of a sauce).

In the autumn of 1959, Gordon C. Cooper of the Tivoli Theatre Circuit signed contracts for Tommy's first tour of Australia. Mr Cooper said it was the "Biggest single deal" in the history of his company: he signed the contract with Tommy over the breakfast table of an unnamed London hotel. Tough negotiations had been ongoing for more than a year. His agent reported that he would be the highest paid British entertainer to visit the Commonwealth.[277] Typical entertainment provided by the 'TIV' was lavish twice-daily reviews, featuring comedians, singers, jugglers, magicians - together with their famous dancers. At that time, most of the capital cities in the individual Australian states had a TIV: acts would tour from theatre to theatre; bringing glamour and excitement.

Tommy must have had his first Christmas off work for three years. But the new year of 1960 saw him recording a new LP - *Get Happy with Tommy* - in front of a crowd of two hundred invited members of his fan club. He had been rehearsing during breaks from filming *Light up the Sky*. One track was the immortal *What a Mouth (what a North and South)*. Tom relates that "I did that record for one person only – my father." Tom went on, "He had said to me, you think you can perform and know

---

[88] Japanese prisoner of war and writer

what you are doing: but until you can sing like the Two Bills from Bermondsey, you've had it." Tommy related that he listened to the Two Bills and thought, "I'm gonna do that."[278] So he did. 7th January Tommy was interviewed on AR's *Close Up* and clips from his films were included.[279]

He flew to Melbourne on the 9th February and played Australia for four months; opening in Melbourne on the 12th. Before that first visit, Tommy said that his aim was to go as far away from the UK as possible. He chose Australia deliberately because, he said, he was virtually unknown there. Technically that was untrue: many people there had bought his records and today many people who were young back in the 1950s remember him well. However, most importantly, both his audiences and he spoke a common language. He was able to make a fresh start with new audiences in his endeavour to learn the craft of an all-round entertainer.

In April, the Sydney Morning Herald reported that 'Tommy Steele rocks Australia.' Having said that, it commented that he wanted 'a big roll' to visit the country: adding that he had 'refused a huge pay off to come to Australia because it was not big enough.' The Morning Herald clearly did not think much of Mr Steele or his financial demands. They reported him as saying that he "Needed to make money quickly" because he felt that his popularity would not last forever. The Herald ended their story saying 'Perhaps the end is closer than he thinks' (which was arguably the worst forecast that the paper ever made).

'Big roll' or not, he was there. One cannot help but wonder whether Tommy Steele's relationship with Australia is one of 'love-hate.' He said, after his first visit, that he played to tough, hard-to-please audiences. It "was purgatory."[280] However, he was learning how to entertain. On the other hand, in an interview with the same Sydney Herald several years later he spoke kindlier of the experience: noting that he had found Australian audiences responsive and easy to warm up. He remembered the people that he met with real affection. Particularly one projectionist at a drive-in cinema who put on an early morning double show just for him.

Tom recalled that he carried the whole second half of the show: appearing in Melbourne (12th February - where he met Maurice Chevalier and put on a sixty-six-minute performance), Brisbane (March 16th - where he was greeted by riotous crowds), Adelaide (7th April) and Sydney (22nd April). In Melbourne he received one of the biggest build ups in local theatre history: added to which he was invited to a garden party at which he was presented to the Governor of Victoria Sir Dallas Brooks resplendent in a top hat. To give him his due the Governor looked really pleased to meet the star.

He noted afterwards that the experience taught him everything that he needed to know about a solo act without a backing group: and, in addition, it taught him how to work with adults instead of screaming teenagers.

Whilst down under he was interviewed on local radio by Binny Lum.[89] The interview took place in the

---

[89] Australian radio and television personality

foyer of a theatre in which he was not appearing: which seemed to amuse her greatly. The interview is the strangest which this writer has heard. Tommy sounds both drowsy and uninterested. At the same time the interviewer adopted a very jolly hockey sticks approach. Maybe he thought her a fool. Perhaps he was right. Be that as it may, he talked about the five weeks he spent filming *Tommy the Toreador* and said that he thought John Kennedy's book was "Fair dinkum."[90]

Overall, the comments that he made then (and since) suggest that the entire experience was something of an ordeal by fire - what businessmen today would call a steep learning curve. However, it probably made him; and when he returned Down Under in 1982, he had made the journey and metamorphosed into one of the world's premier song and dance men.

Eventually Tommy returned from Australia for the arguably good reason that he had arranged to get married. Notwithstanding that the NME reported on 27th May that the romance was on the rocks. Presumably not for Richardson noted that he and Ann were busy fixing up their home to-be on the River Thames. It was, she reported, an old coach house where the London-Bristol mail coach used to pull up. She noted that he intended to buy a small inconspicuous car in which to travel to and from work.[281]

Going back for a moment, in autumn 1959 a contract had been exchanged for an eighteen-week season at Blackpool Opera House with Harry Robinson and his

---

[90] Australian slang meaning confirmation of the truth of something.

Orchestra (sadly the Steelmen were never to be engaged again): it was to be his first major summer season. After his marriage, which we shall come to in a moment, he was to translate to Blackpool for what was to be a highly praised and very successful summer season. He planned to present the act that he developed on his Australian tour.

Before the show started, he was scheduled to appear on the BBC Ivor Novello Awards programme on Monday 6th June to collect his Award for the year's Outstanding Novelty Item - *Little White Bull*. His management pulled him from the show at the last minute allegedly because he was not going to receive the actual Award during the programme: one of many disputes between Steele and various organizations at that time. To the great disappointment of his fans his place was taken by Ronnie Carroll: it was a public relations disaster.

Meanwhile he married on 18th June at St Patrick's Roman Catholic church Soho. His wedding reception was held at the Savoy Hotel River Room: there were three hundred guests. Colour film of the event was included in that week's Pathé News. It was dubbed *the show business wedding of the year.* Colin Hicks was best man and flew in from Italy. The bride's sister Kathleen burst into tears outside the church. Leo Pollini and Alan Stuart were there: as were John Le Mesurier, Jimmy Edwards and Alma Cogan. Fifty policemen - mounted and on foot - formed a cordon to keep the crowd back.[282] What excitement! But imagine the cost to the public purse.

The Big Show of 1960 established Tommy as an all-round entertainer; although NME reported that he lacked the easy repose of an accomplished artiste: when all was said and done, he was still learning. He appeared three times during the course of the show (which co-stared Alma Cogan) singing and dancing. 19th September he appeared on Tyne Tees *Star Parade* and immediately after the show Tommy began rehearsals for his much-anticipated appearance in *She Stoops to Conquer* at the Old Vic.

While Tommy was appearing in Melbourne, the Old Vic Director Michael Benthall had an inspiration. Benthall had seen Tom in *Cinderella* at the London Coliseum and thought him 'One of the most professional performers' that he had ever seen. The Observer noted that 'a kind of magic prevailed when Steele performed on stage and that he had a great feeling for the mood of the audience.'[283] Ellis noted that this was a quality that most stars lacked.[284] Tommy himself had mentioned to DISC that he had "Learned to play to an audience and hold them but now I want to discover HOW to do it."[285]

Benthall's inspiration led to a moment of history. He wrote to Tommy inviting him to appear at the Old Vic. Simultaneously Tommy received an invitation to star in Billy Liar. With the benefit of hindsight either choice might have taken him to fresh heights away from rock 'n' roll. So, Tommy announced that he had chosen the Old Vic. As he famously commented to the BBC, he went to the Old Vic "To learn: not to earn" still regarding himself as an apprentice in the business. He confessed to NME a year later that when he first read the script he could not understand where the laughs were: a steep learning curve indeed. It was rumoured that that he turned down £2000 a week (a fortune in 1960: and not bad money now) to earn £60 per week on the Waterloo Road. Tommy told DISC "Financially of course it means nothing"[286] he might not have said that if he had still been a £10 a week sailor. Speaking of the whole thing more than fifty years later he said that his agent was dead against it: and that simply through spite Parnes insisted on receiving his percentage. A comment that perhaps tells us something of what he thought of Mr Parnes, Shillings and Pence.

The play was presented for five performances a week; enabling Tommy to prepare for his Christmas Day show on ATV. Eric Sykes[91] was asked to write the script for this ninety-minute festive show. It was set for recording on 20th December and in it he was due to be re-united with his Old Vic co-star the formidable Peggy Mount.[92] While rehearsing he was settling into his new home.

He opened at the Old Vic on 8th November. His role was Tony Lumpkin. The part was originally written for a Mr Woodward a famous comedian of his day: so historically it was intended to be a humorous part: it was certainly not written for a vocalist. His step-sister Kate was played by Judi Dench: she remarked that at first Tommy seemed scared of working with those he perceived to be grand classical actors: but that this concern was ameliorated somewhat by the friendship that he struck up with old Etonian Nicholas Meredith (legend

---

[91] Popular comedian and television script writer
[92] English actress well known for playing stubborn and argumentative women

has it that they often ate together in Tommy's favourite eel and pie shop).

The production's Director Douglas Seale asked Tommy how he planned to play Tony Lumpkin. Surprised at the question, Tom responded that "He would play him as a northerner" - as that was what he was. Ironically, the play had never been set in the north before. The Director thought this a splendid idea.

The appearance of Britain's original rock 'n' roll idol on the hallowed ground of the Old Vic certainly caused a stir. NME's Derek Johnson suggested that some of his gestures and grimaces were overplayed. He wrote 'I do not think that Tommy's Tony Lumpkin is quite what Goldsmith envisaged. However, full credit to him therefore that he has adapted the role to fit his own personality. He literally romps through the part; bubbling with enthusiasm. Never once did he seem out of place.'[287]

Journalist Betty Best commented that there was only one member of the cast who meant anything to the kids in the audience: she noted wryly that the player concerned probably had his own pavement hopscotch pitch around the corner less than fifteen years before. If anyone had ever suggested to Tommy at *that* time that he would one day star at the Old Vic (a theatre that he himself described to American LIFE magazine some years later as "The severest of repertory mills")[288] he would probably have said "Knock it mate: that's for squares."

But his fans packed the gallery to see a play of which many of them might never have heard. Judi Dench reported that many fans were unsure of what they were going to see. She recalls the story that one fan sent in a note asking him to sing *Little White Bull* in celebration of 'Our Maudie's birthday.' He had a dictionary by his side and looked up every word that he did not understand.[289] Although the stuffy Old Vic regulars thought the whole caper a bit of a casting gimmick, the reviews made Tommy's financial sacrifice worthwhile. Sir John Betjeman rose to applaud his Tony Lumpkin:[290] what a decent think for the future Poet Laurate to do.

Beyond that, the decision to go and 'learn' suggested that he was - as he always has been - one of the wisest and most level headed people in show business. One unnamed paper (quoted in the Independent years later) saw the comedy as an affectionate and warm-hearted production with the unexpected casting of Tommy Steele as Tony Lumpkin and thought it 'larkily successful.' It was a personal triumph. He took fourteen curtain calls and brought the house down: the morning after he had pictures in every newspaper. The Daily Telegraph opined that he could speak a line with point and intelligence and display exuberant high spirits. The Times suggested that he was conscientiously learning to be a straight actor: not surprisingly, Michael Benthall asked him to play another season.[291]

30th November, by kind permission of the Directors of the Old Vic Trust (which is how they used to write in those days), Tommy starred in a special edition of *London Lights*[93] in the Concert Hall of Broadcasting

---

[93] A Commonwealth Gala

House. It was aired on the BBC's Light programme to mark the London Commonwealth Exhibition.

On 11th December Tommy missed a signal honour (and not a lot of people know this). John Freeman[94] had achieved lasting fame for his one-to-one interviews with famous people: *Face to Face*. He was regarded as the doyen of interviewers. He had determined to include Tommy Steele as one of his guests – representing the younger generation. However, his step-daughter Lisa dissuaded him and, at her special request, Freeman interviewed Adam Faith instead.[292]

Christmas Day, Tommy turned up at the Savoy Hotel - having enjoyed his wedding reception there so much - dressed as Father Christmas.[293] He was also on television that day on ITV in the *Tommy Steele Show - The Squire*. This had a mediaeval theme with Tommy playing a Squire and with Bernard Cribbins playing a Baron. Tommy sang seven songs.[294]

Following *She Stoops to Conquer* (the run having ended at the end of December) Tommy and Ann flew to Bermuda. They then made their way to Barbados, Jamaica, Trinidad, Venezuela and Curaçao. They flew over Cuba and ended up in New York: six weeks in all: a very long delayed honeymoon (he told the NME that he had wanted to show his wife the places that he had visited while on the ships).

Tom related a singular story to DISC. He claimed that, while in New York, he had arranged to visit former

---

[94] One-time British Ambassador to the United States

colleagues on the *Mauretania*. He was forbidden entry to the ship by security who asked to see his permit. He had none. The duty officer refused to let him use the liner's ship-to-shore radio to confirm permission to board. So, he took a cab to the shipping office and obtained a permit. On producing the permit, the officer still would not let him board the ship. Then the duty officer accidently fell into the water (as one does). The officer pulled himself out of the water and took a swipe at Tommy. The tale had a happy ending as Tom's former mates came off the ship and met him ashore.[295] Mr and Mrs Hicks returned around the 3rd February 1961; both must have felt that it was a well-earned break.

In March Tom appeared in ATV's *Saturday Spectacular*; thereafter he signed a new five-year contract with Parnes. Then his first national tour since November 1958 saw him kicking off at the Stockton Globe: NME reported that it was his old songs that were the best received. This Granada tour - at a myriad of diverse theatres from Dartford to Walthamstow! - was to keep him on the stage for much of 1961. When he appeared at Taunton - for a whole week (there was never going to be enough local demand to fill the old Gaumont for a week) - he stayed at the then County Hotel. A local youth, Chris Mitchell, was engaged to sleep on the floor outside his room to prevent any local lasses trying to break in (such is the price of fame).

This extended tour took him through until the end of June. Writing in NME that month, Don Wedge commented that one year after his marriage Tommy had completed a 'proving year:' marked by his appearance on

Sunday Night at the London Palladium on 11th June – his first appearance on the show since 5th January 1958; three and a half years before. Tommy considered that the metamorphous began with his long summer season at Blackpool in 1960. Tom then appeared at the Grand Opera House Belfast for five days starting on 12th June.

Meanwhile on the same date a photograph appeared in the press of the President of the Bermondsey Boat Club – none other than Tommy Steele – relaxing at his Thames side house at Lower Teddington Road, Hampton Wick. The caption advised that he had an old lamppost from Bermondsey (one that actually worked) in his garden. The picture showed Tommy and his motor launch named *Yogi Bear* tied up to his private slipway.[296] On the same date the BBC featured him on *a World of Sound* introduced by Desmond Carrington: who was to remain an admirer until his death in 2017.

On 25th June Tommy appeared on *Val Parnell's Sunday Show*[95] and the next day he commenced a summer season at the Windmill Theatre Great Yarmouth which ended on 16th September. It was the first summer season at the Windmill and Frankie Howard was also on the bill. Owner Jack Jay said it cost him a fortune to get Tommy commenting that he had to get two capacity shows each night to make the show pay for itself. He said: "The Tommy Steele people held out for a very high figure – I could not beat them down."[297] You bet he could not beat down Parnes, Shillings and Pence. Tommy had great respect for Frankie Howard and insisted that he take the

---

[95] Summer replacement for *Sunday Night at the Sunday Palladium*

star's dressing room even though he himself was top of the bill. Frankie never forgot that kindness.

While there, upgraded from a caravan, he and Ann rented a house on the Lowestoft Road and drove around in a Morris Minor. One highlight was that *The Tommy Steele Story* was being shown in town and he, Bruce Forsyth and Gary Miller[96] were photographed coming out of the cinema: all having watched the film.[298] 25th June he was back on ITV starring in Val Parnell's Sunday Show *The Tommy Steele Hour*. It was an all-period-costume satirical show focussed on the Battle of Waterloo.[299]

On Sunday 27th August Tommy headed a strong bill on BBC *Seaside Nights* with Emile Ford and his Checkmates: featuring those appearing in Great Yarmouth that summer. It was recorded at the Wellington Pier Theatre. Very unusually the annual Church Service for Show Business Stars of Great Yarmouth Summer Shows was held at St. James' Church in Great Yarmouth. Can you imagine it happening today? There was a full congregation; Bob Monkhouse and Tommy Steele each read a lesson. Bruce Forsyth and Frankie Howard among others were sidesmen.[300]

Tom enjoyed a three-week break after his season at the Windmill. Autumn 1961 witnessed a strange happening: Lionel Bart recorded and issued[97] *Give us a kiss for Christmas*. Now, here's the thing. Bart wrote it for Tommy Steele (and had everything gone to plan it would

---

[96] A popular vocalist in the '50s and '60s who died young from a heart attack
[97] On Decca F-11405

have been Tommy's last Bart-written release). Bart turned up at the recording studios and waited for Tommy's arrival. Save that he did not arrive. Bart got fed up with waiting and recorded the song himself (and he was no singer). It would have cost Tommy a lot in lost sales. The story went that at the end of October Tommy motored to Kingston Upon Thames to be fitted for pantomime clothes to be used in Liverpool two months later. Tom claimed that a part-time secretary got dates mixed up. Bart decided to make a demonstration record of the way he wanted his song recorded and Decca liked it so much that they decided to release it. It *was* voted a hit on *Juke Box Jury* and sold 10,000 copies (to Bart's benefit).[301]

After his much-needed three-week break, he started rehearsals at the Coventry Theatre[98] on 9th October (before commencing a seven-week run on 17th) starring in S. H. Newsome's *Birthday Show*. It ended on 2nd December. In the show, he took off Joy Beverley in a skit on the Beverley Sisters.[99] It was the first recorded time that he introduced *Speed Maniacs*: an act combining film and live action that he continued to use right through until the 1990s.

The programme commented that 'not only was this his first appearance in the city for three years, but in the intervening time Tommy had developed into an accomplished entertainer far beyond rock 'n' roll.' At this very time, October 1961, NME made the first report of the

---

[98] Sam Newsome's Hippodrome became the Coventry Theatre (*The Showplace of The Midlands*); and later became again the Apollo
[99] Who were not in the show!

possible production of Half a Sixpence. This is interesting because Tommy always relates that he first heard part of the score whilst appearing later in pantomime in Liverpool. On Friday 10th November he appeared with Sir John Gielgud in a *Great All-Star Midnight Matinee* in aid of the Coventry Cathedral Festival (at which he reprised *Speed Maniacs* with Vanessa Redgrave).

It was then that fire and thunder nearly involved the star. Tom's manager, John Kennedy, lived at Wraysbury. He was in turn also agent for actor Sid James.[100] He staged a fireworks party for the stars of show business: it turned into a night of horror in which three people died: David Scott (26) a male model, Hilda Parsons a mother of two little girls, and barrister Michael Talbot (49), who died from a heart attack after escaping from the flames. The next day the £8,000 bungalow was a heap of charred ruins and police were questioning the sixty guests to find out how it happened. The outcome was that fire had swept through the timber-built home on a Thames island after a huge pile of fireworks were set alight. They had been stored in an upturned umbrella on the patio (not perhaps the most sensible place to keep them). Sid James bravely fought his way back into the burning house no less than three times to get people out.[302] He was taken to Slough hospital where he had a severe cut to his hand stitched and dressed.

Kennedy was a bit of a goer. So, I suspect was John Edwards who, you will remember, was Tommy's Tour Manager on some of the early tours. Kennedy's

---

[100] Co-star of Hancock's Half Hour

home was only fifteen miles from the Cliveden home of the third Viscount Astor. The Bohemian artist and osteopath Stephen Ward rented a weekend cottage on the Cliveden Estate down by the lake. He invited Edwards and Kennedy to weekend parties there. Ward liked the company of famous people. Kennedy turned up at one party with his current date, Jill Browne, who played nurse Carole Young in the hugely popular TV series *Emergency Ward Ten*. Diana Dors turned up with a gangster[303] (she knew about gangsters). Knightley and Kennedy relate that one weekend Tommy Steele was invited for the afternoon. He lost his way (Cliveden is difficult to find). He stopped his car in front of an impressive gateway and said to a man standing just inside "Excuse me, do you know how to get to Cliveden?" "Yes," the man replied "Straight in here but you have to pay an entrance fee of 2/-." Tommy paid and found the cottage. Later Viscount Astor visited the cottage. Ward introduced Tommy to him. "Ah", Tommy said "You are the man who took my 2/-. Do you mind if I have it back?"[304]

Before proceeding to Liverpool there was a rare airing of the film *Kill me Tomorrow* on 6th December in which he had made a cameo appearance *and* there was a Christmas Day special for ATV. In those far off days Christmas was not complete without Tommy Steele on television. He returned to the Liverpool Empire for Christmas 1961 to appear in *Humpty Dumpty*: rehearsals started on 11th December and he opened on 23rd for a ten-week run ending on the 3rd March. In an interview with *LatestBrighton*,[305] Tommy described this as "The worst show I ever did in my life." He recalled that he went to the London Palladium to see Harry Secombe fill the role two years before. At the beginning of the show the egg fell off the castle wall and cracked open and out climbed Harry Secombe. When Tommy got to Liverpool nobody knew how the mechanism for the falling egg worked and the guy who created it had left. Tom commented that "I ended up doing twelve weeks hating the opening because I just had to walk on." Notwithstanding this, NME rated the show a big hit describing Tommy as being at his sparkling best. Whilst there, he represented the Variety Artistes' Club when he opened the new Play Centre on Grenville Street.[306]

Every cloud has a silver lining. In the fourth week of the run Harold Fielding called him about a new show. "He wanted me to hear it and said that, if I liked it, he would produce it." So, the composer David Heneker, writer Beverley Cross and his girlfriend Maggie Smith came up to Liverpool (the latter to read the girl part); Tom said "She was such a beautiful woman." So, it came to pass that *Half a Sixpence* was born. Tommy immediately agreed to do it: it was an obvious career move. As they would say today, it 'was a no brainer.' His infectious enthusiasm and personality were to make him an ideal musical comedy star.[307]

7th January 1962 Tommy appeared again on Val Parnell's *Sunday Night at The London Palladium*: and it is disillusioning to think that this writer saw the programme and remembers it as though it was yesterday. It was hosted by Norman Vaughan who was compèring the show for the first time. The orchestrations for Tommy performance had been left in a taxi: they arrived eventually after being handed in at a police station. Tommy sang *Wishing Star* which was written by Ronnie Carroll:[101] on the broadcast Tommy referred to Carroll as "That well-known IRA specialist"[308] which may or may not have gone down well. Tommy had recorded the number but it was never issued as a single: which is no surprise as it was dreary.

There is discussion concerning other recorded, but unreleased, tracks made about this time. Tatham[102] noted that he had recorded *Green Eye, Setting the Woods on Fire* and *My Bucket's Got a Hole In It*[309] and there are long held beliefs that he also recorded *Volare* (and there is certainly a demo in existence of *One Times One)*.[103] Tom's A & R man at Decca, Hugh Mendl, eventually - and probably not helped by his capacity for cigarettes - suffered a serious heart attack in 1979 at the British Phonographic Industry Christmas party. He attributed this to "The stress of working for a dying company." The Independent reported that whilst he was convalescing, the new owners of Decca cleared Mendl's office, throwing away his diaries ~ which represented a valuable de facto history of Decca. We can assume that with this carnage, any such unreleased pressings would have been destroyed.

In June, The Record Mirror reported that comedian Stan Stennett had been giving Tommy flying lessons. He commented later that he had found the noise of the engines deafened his ear drums: so, he packed it in.[310]

---

[101] A popular singer born in Belfast
[102] Dick Tatham was a music journalist for Record Mirror and Disc
[103] Decca Matrix DRF 28736

High flyer though he undoubtedly was, nothing more was ever heard again of this pastime.

23rd June Tommy appeared on *Thank your Lucky Stars*: it was his first appearance on a 'pop' show since November 1958. His mission appeared to be to promote his cover of Brook Benton's *Hit Record*. On 13th July, Norman Jopling, a writer for Record Mirror, savaged the record making the point that it was not even a hit for the American originator. Tommy seemed much taken with the song, which a number of people felt was the worst record that he ever made: and a misjudgement to boot. It was played on *Juke Box Jury* and one panel member, visiting American Johnny Mathis[104], subjected the track to a blast of criticism that echoed around Britain. Many viewers were offended by what Mathis – a guest in this country - said: and the way that he said it.[311] He remained unapologetic.

Meanwhile, Tommy recorded three more shows for ATV. One was *The Steele Hour* for Bernard Delfont's *Sunday Show* which broadcast on 8th July. *The Hour* featured what Tommy believed was the longest dance routine ever seen on television at that time. He was joined in it by co-stars Norman Vaughan[105] (with whom he had not worked before) and Jeannie Carson.[106] It was called *Steam Heat* from the *Pyjama Game*.[107]

---

[104] Well known and up-market singer, songwriter
[105] Comedian and show presenter
[106] Singer and dancer with a star in Hollywood's Walk of Fame
[107] Broadway musical opened 1954

His performance in another - *A Show of Steele* – broadcast on Sunday 12th August - was described as that of a brilliant consummate artiste, a far cry from rock 'n' roll. However, it is noted that complaints were made concerning Tommy lip synching to existing recordings – he sang *In an English Country Garden* and *Inchworm* (with children from The Corona Stage School) among others.[312] The third, broadcast on 2nd September, was *Some of Steele* (by then it was almost a handful of Steele).

Another honour was that he was invited to star in the first *City of London Festival*; appearing on television on 9th July with his old cobber Sir John Gielgud and John Betjeman. The latter wrote - and helped produce - a masque which was performed before the Queen at the Mansion House.[313] The Daily Mail wrote that 'It needed Tommy Steele to melt the ice. He exploded onto the stage: he sang one song and a leaden audience twitched into life:'[314] that song was *What a Mouth (what a North and South)*: the man, who was rapidly becoming a polymath, also read poetry. Interestingly, McHugh refers to his 'forthcoming collection of poetry' at the time of the filming of *Sixpence*. One wonders what happened to *that*.[315] The *City of London* programme was televised and broadcast that same evening.

He appeared in Sunday concerts at the Blackpool Opera House on 22nd July, 5th August and 19th August. In the programme for his two appearances at the Bournemouth Winter Gardens on the 12th and 26th August the notes quote a then recent column in the Daily Express in which a journalist commented 'Unlike the ghostly host of rock 'n' rollers, Tommy Steele will be in business for the next fifty years.' The writer might have written 'sixty.' The notes continued 'He is sure of his place in the Hall of Fame along with Harry Lauder, Marie Lloyd and Gracie Fields.' Praise indeed for a young man not yet aged twenty-six still learning his trade: and this was 1962.

By now Tommy Steele was not just a hot ticket but also a hot rod. He was fined £25 (which one suspects he could afford) for driving on a stretch of the not long opened M1 at 120 mph and overtaking on the inside lane. He announced that he was selling the 3.8 L Jaguar.

5th October came the announcement that he was leaving Decca and moving to Columbia records. Tommy flew to Dusseldorf for an important charity event supporting UNICEF on 17th October (postponed from 21st September). Highlights from this event were eventually broadcast by the BBC on 7th July the following year – and although top billed[316] Tommy's contribution was cut out due to a contractual issue with ATV. Later Tommy appeared in *Down Home in South London*, a BBC radio programme featuring early reminiscences from him and, in addition, fellow Londoners Billy Cotton, Tommy Trinder, Arthur Haynes and Charlie Drake. All names from the distant past.

A little remembered Blackpool visit saw Tommy topping a variety bill at the old Queen's Theatre for the last two weeks of the summer season in October in James Brennan's *You'll See Stars*. NME reported that an energy-charged Tommy Steele leapt onto the stage and threw himself into the star spot. Few people present would have realized that after touring almost nonstop as a rock 'n' roll singer for two years and then touring as a variety entertainer in Australia, UK and Scandinavia for a similar length of time that this was to be the last occasion that he was to appear on the stage as a song and dance man until he opened in Las Vegas in 1970. By that time, he really had become a seasoned entertainer.

2nd November NME reported filming was to start just before Christmas on *It's All Happening*. Tommy's role was to be that of an A and R Manager. Production started late, as they decided to shoot it in colour. It was announced that the Director was to be Kenneth Hume:[108] in the event it was directed by Don Sharp, who shot the film *The Golden Disc* for the ill-fated Terry Dene. The film was made in six weeks: and a pretty poor film it was too. Tommy celebrated Christmas with the issue of *He's Got Love*: his last issue as a pop singer on Decca and one of the best of his own compositions. After filming started Tommy topped the bill at the London Palladium on Friday 23rd November in *The Midnight Stars*. Midnight charity events were very popular in that era – perhaps they jazzed up what was otherwise a rather dull era. This early morning extravaganza was in aid of the East London Spastic Society Clinic Centre Building Fund. The show was produced once again by Ernest Maxim and also featured among many others Hattie Jacques and Ian Carmichael.

In an interview with NME Tommy called 1962 "His TV year." It concluded magnificently with ATV

---

[108] Then husband of Shirley Bassey

broadcasting *The Tommy Steele Show: Quincy's Quest* on 23rd December. It was a seminal event for Tommy. Written by Tommy - and also featuring Una Stubbs and Hugh Paddick - the story related how unwanted toys in a department store were set to be destroyed. One of the rejects, a doll named Quincy, went on a quest to find Santa Claus who it believed was the only person who might save them all. This show was so successful that Tommy developed it into a major film seventeen years later. It was remembered for years by many young viewers.

So, 1963 saw Tommy Steele filming at Shepperton - with location filming in Richmond Theatre - from where he proceeded to rehearse for the blockbuster that was to change his life. One of the songs *The Dream Maker* backed with *Maximum Plus* was released only as a Demo. It was reviewed favourably but not issued: although copies remain. There are various stories concerning why it was pulled: one is that his managers wanted both tracks to feature Tommy Steele alone. Another is that Tommy objected to having a song coupled with Marion Ryan[109] on its flip side: and he threatened to leave Columbia (presumably he would have had to share royalties with Ryan). EMI referred to 'a technical problem.' The company hastily replaced the flipside with *Egg and Chips*. As it was one of only two records of his issued by Columbia one might conclude that his (brief) relationship with the company was not very happy. Incidentally, the film was released as *The Dream Maker* in parts of the United States.

---

[109] Popular singer at the time who appeared with him in the film

On 19th February Tommy appeared on ATV's *Sing A Song for Sixpence: Fall of the Curtain* when - third in a series of three - Sir John Betjeman reflected on the English Music Hall.

CHAPTER FOUR

THE VOYAGE TO BROADWAY

Rehearsals for *Half a Sixpence* - in which NME reported that RCA-Victor[110] had made a substantial investment (it was the first time that an American record company had invested in a British show) - commenced on 6th February: and an advertisement appeared for 'Boy and Girl dancers' for the production with auditions at the Scala Theatre[111] on 1st February 1963.

Rehearsals came to a stop at one point when Tommy had to give evidence at Hampstead Magistrates Court in a case in which three people were accused of conspiracy to defraud. A letter had been sent to his bank asking for £980 to be released bearing a forgery of his signature. He appeared in court to confirm that the signature on the letter was a forgery.[317] It must have been an unwanted diversion.

However, work had started one year before. On 13th March 1962 demo recordings for *Kipps*[112] (as it was then planned to name the musical) were made at Olympic Studios in Barnes. Both Tommy and his understudy[113]

---

[110] Now owned by Sony
[111] Demolished in 1969
[112] The Story of a Simple Soul, 1905
[113] Roy Sone

took part: they include several songs that were dropped subsequently.

Previews for the musical were staged at the Wimbledon Theatre for six days: with the World Première on Saturday 9th March 1963. While at Wimbledon quite a few changes were made to perfect the production. Every ticket had been sold three weeks before the trial run started. The manager at Wimbledon (who banned all but local critics) described it as "The biggest success we have ever had."[318] Larry Parnes was quoted as saying "Tommy Steele is a sensation; unbelievably good;" although a cynic might comment that he would say that. NME quoted the Surrey Comet saying that 'Tommy Steele was H. G. Wells' hero to the life'.

The London opening was at the Cambridge Theatre on 21st March. Although Bernard Levin[114] characteristically managed to make snide remarks, Sir Harold Hobson doyen of British critics wrote 'with a full recognition of the enormity of the statement, Mr Steele's performance is the best I have ever seen in a musical; it is the most varied and the most penetrating. Over and over again he astounds with the truth of his emotion, the exactness of his observation. Perfection is rare: I doubt if we shall ever see anything like this again.' Once again, this was heady stuff. Another critic wrote "Cor what a bloomin' triumph."[319] One unknown critic opined 'Mr Steele reminds us of something that we had almost

---

[114] **Times** journalist: described as 'the most famous journalist of his day'

forgotten: that at the centre of a musical there can be a positive personality and a star performance.'

However, The Telegraph, writing in the effortlessly superior metro-liberal languid manner adopted by some very superior beings, suggested that the musical was 'A period pantomime' with Kipps as 'Buttons in a boater.' It continued, 'Tommy Steele - with his candy-floss mop of hair and orange peel teeth - gives his usual spirited performance and engaging impersonation of a rock 'n' roll Bugs Bunny.'[115] Eric Shorter referred to the 'pleasant, tousled toothy charm of Tommy Steele.'[320]

There is an interesting story behind the show's big hit. Tommy relates that: "Three days before the show opened the producers were worried that there was no big number in the second act. It is what they call the *eleven o'clock number* on Broadway as it's the song that the audience goes out talking about it. Summoned to the theatre for rehearsal on the Sunday before the show opened, the composer David Heneker announced that he had the song. He sat down at the little piano and played *Flash, Bang, Wallop!*[116] and that was our big number: with only two days before the show opened the choreographer said there was no way he could do a dance routine for the whole company. He solved the problem by keeping movement to a minimum."

The scene was in a photographer's studio where Arthur Kipps had gone to discuss his wedding. There's a line in the chorus that goes 'Hold it, Flash, Bang, Wallop,

---

[115] Animated cartoon rabbit
[116] Which became a new phrase in the English language

what a picture' so Tommy was told to run up and down singing it like a pub song and every time he sang 'Hold It' the cast froze into funny positions: and it worked. Hopefully nobody noticed the photographer had the words of the song pinned underneath his camera so Tommy could read them: there was no time to learn them properly.

When the show opened the audience went wild. "There was so much applause" he says "that when we went off stage to change for the next scene, they were still clapping: so, we had to come back to take a bow to stop them so the show could carry on."[321]

When the show opened his managers and agent invited members of the Tommy Steele Fan Club to lunch; along with Tommy's wife and parents. In spite of his move to Columbia, Decca cut the LP of the show. The A & R man being Hugh Mendl who had worked on Tom's first disc in 1956. *Half a Sixpence* also featured Marti Webb playing Ann in her first leading role. The production was directed by John Dexter, with choreography by Edmund Balin. The set was designed, once again, by Loudon Sainthill. It ran for 677 performances. 'It was a personal triumph for Tommy Steele' wrote Patrick Boyle in the Spectator.[322] Critics spoke of Tommy's natural talent and charisma.[323] One unknown critic of Half a Sixpence wrote of Tommy's performance 'with an eye roll here and an eye roll there, here a grin there a grin, everywhere a high kick he fairly wallops us into loving him.' McHugh refers to Tommy flashing his trademark toothy grin[324] in a review of the film of Sixpence.

'House Full' signs went up at the end the first week – and stayed up. Within three months NME was reporting that the show was fully booked for a whole year.[325] Sunday 7th April Tommy and co-star Marti Webb appeared on the BBC Light programme in *Show Time '63* with highlights from the programme. By July, Tommy had been voted Musical Actor of the Year by London theatre critics; however, 24th May saw Tommy out of the show for two days with throat trouble.

A nice story emerged from the London run. Reported in the *Daily Telegraph* it concerned Barbara Sargent; a blind telephonist. Barbara turned up at the Cambridge Theatre with eighty of her office colleagues; together with her guide dog, Merry. The dog could not be admitted. She had to sit in a nearby coffee bar while her friends enjoyed the show. The company manager heard about the incident and told Tommy. He arranged for her to return later in the week and sit in the Royal Box – which had its own private staircase to which Merry was allowed access. There were flowers and chocolates waiting for her on her arrival and she joined the star in his dressing room after the show for a champagne supper: *and* there was freshly cooked meat for Merry.[326]

On 19th April, Tommy appeared on ITV's programme *Close Up on British Musicals* and talked about his new movie *It's All Happening:* one imagines that there was nothing measurable to say about it. Then on the 18th June, Tommy was banned from driving for a year and fined £30 at West London Magistrates Court for driving at a dangerous speed on the Great West Road. It was stated that he had two previous convictions (£10 fine in Great Yarmouth 1961; £25 fine + £30 costs in Luton 1962 when driving a Jaguar, which he sold subsequently). On this occasion, he was observed on 2nd March driving his M.G.B. sports car[117] at 90 m.p.h. over the Hammersmith Flyover in West London. He had overtaken two policemen:[327] as well as five cars on the inside:[118] not the most sensible thing to do. He claimed to have been in a hurry as he had overslept; and was on his way to rehearsals. That evening he borrowed a bike and went for a trial spin.[328]

Half a Sixpence was to dominate his life for two years. However, he appeared in an interview on *Close Up* on 23rd August and 15th September also saw him headlining the first of the new series of *Sunday Night at the London Palladium* (for what was to be his last appearance on the show), compèred by Bruce Forsyth. Tommy was joined by the cast of *Half a Sixpence*. Further, on 2nd October he appeared on the BBC's Light Programme in *Let's Find Out* when he answered unscripted and unrehearsed questions from a panel of teenagers.

In the same month he was out of the show for several days with a strained tendon, which involved his seeing a specialist, and his part was taken over by understudy Roy Sone. One can understand why his contract for *Half a Sixpence* included a 'no football'

---

[117] It was wrongly suggested that this was the MG that featured in *Tommy the Toreador* and which was owned by Tommy Steele Enterprises Ltd. He had bought the M.G.B. new in October 1962 for £1150.
[118] Peter Senn reported in the Daily Mirror

clause. This would have been a considerable sacrifice for Tommy: playing centre forward was one of his passions (and he was good at it). Incidentally, the Show Biz XI for which he was a leading light often trained at Highbury Stadium.[119/329]

4th November saw Tommy in his second *Royal Variety Performance* (this time at the Prince of Wales Theatre) together with the cast of *Half a Sixpence*. The Performance was timed so that *Sixpence* could continue as scheduled that evening. Impresario Richard Mills recalls that he stopped the show: forty-one years later at the *Royal Variety Performance* in 2004, at the age of sixty-eight, he did so again.[330]

29th December saw his first ever radio series on the BBC Light Programme: this ran (almost without a break) through until 29th March 1964. The programme was to be a mixture of music and happy chat: he had cut a pilot towards the end of 1963. The Raindrops and the Johnnie Spence Orchestra were also featured. It replaced the *Billy Cotton Band Show*: and proved to be good light entertainment; if not epoch breaking. One break was in January when Tommy was ordered to rest and he and his wife went to the West Indies: he was warned that if he did not do this, he risked having a nervous breakdown. Pre-recording of the radio show took place at the Playhouse Theatre.

It is interesting to note that there were several occasions when Tommy was ordered to take it easy. However, in between all the excitements, the 3rd August

---

[119] Until 2006 home of Arsenal Football Club

1964 saw BBC radio broadcasting The Tommy Steele Show *Tommy at the Fair*. Two months later on 31st October *Half a Sixpence* closed at the Cambridge Theatre and the star went on a two-month holiday. He must have been drained. Whilst he was away on the 29th November BBC broadcast a tribute to Winston Churchill just before his 90th birthday. Tom starred along with Frankie Vaughan and Alma Cogan. A month later, it was announced that Tommy was to star in a second series of his BBC radio shows.

Yet again Tommy starred at Christmas for ATV - his first television show of the year. It was his last appearance on British television for a very long time because he was about to leave for Broadway. The show was *Richard Whittington Esquire* broadcast on Rediffusion on Christmas Day. He wrote the story and starred as Dick Whittington: a role he was to reprise with distinction at the Palladium five years later. A complete surviving 16mm film recording of this show was sold on eBay in 2016.[331]

On 13th January 1965 Tommy sailed to the US to begin rehearsals for what was ultimately to be his Broadway debut. Whether he consciously realized it or not, this voyage marked the end of one era; and the beginning of another in his life as an entertainer. He sailed away from the UK as a young man who had morphed from rock 'n' roll singer to family entertainer; with a great London theatre success under his belt (he was described as 'Britain's leading young comedy musical star' in the New York Programme notes). His ongoing experiences in the New World saw his conversion to an internationally respected star of stage and screen and within two or three years he would become a different person.

Actually, the show nearly failed to make Broadway. Remember that the hit song was *Flash, Bang, Wallop!* The American producers said they had to drop the song because the Americans would not understand it. But Tommy was having none of it. He told them that the show went with the song or it did not go at all. He won. *Flash, Bang, Wallop!* stayed in the show and the American audiences lapped it up.[332] Having said that, a few of the songs were deemed unsuitable for American audiences and were dropped.[333]

Following Tommy's arrival in the US, ABC announced it would broadcast four hour-long specials sponsored by the Aluminum Company of America. However, only two were ever broadcast before the sponsor dropped the project. Both the shows that *were* broadcast were hosted by Douglas Fairbanks Jr: both giving viewers a behind-the-scenes look at the world of entertainment. The second programme was *Watch it. With Douglas Fairbanks Junior.*[334] It was broadcast on Sunday 14th March – just before Tommy opened in Boston. It featured Brigitte Bardot, Jack Lemmon, Virna Lisa, Florence Eldridge, Fredric March, and Tommy Steele.

There was a trial run of *Half a Sixpence* at the Colonial Theatre Boston[120] from the week of 15th March. This was followed by a second trial at the O'Keefe Centre for the Performing Arts[121] in Toronto - a 3200 seat

---

[120] Now the Emerson Colonial Theatre
[121] Now the Meridian Hall

auditorium - from Tuesday 30th March to 17th April. Here the programme described Tommy for the first time as a 'living legend:' he must have felt that he had arrived. NME reported that the audience applauded constantly. Richardson quotes Dave Clifford writing that 'the audience showed their approval in a manner rarely seen in sedate Canada. Tommy Steele earned thunderous waves of applause and is 1965's big new star. The critics stood and applauded: something they last did for Danny Kaye.'[335]

Tommy opened on Broadway on 25th April where he was to play at the Broadhurst Theatre for 511 performances. *Half a Sixpence* was the last West End show to transfer successfully to New York City until the late 1970s. Reviews were generally favourable. LIFE reported 'the best hoofing[122] of the year, infectious songs and a bravura performance by Steele who flashes a smile so dazzling that the theatre scarcely needs footlights.'[336] The extent - and sincerity - of his smile was to prove controversial for fifty years: however, his agent was quoted as saying "That smile is worth a million pounds to him."[337]

The Daily News opined 'the musical should lighten anybody's heart.' The New York Times described him as 'a song and dance man whose mastery is currently unsurpassed by any other performer' but was underwhelmed by the show's intellectual content describing it as 'friendly wholesome corn' whilst the normally aggressive Herald Tribune wrote that the star 'can do a bit of everything a bit better than most:' not bad

---

[122] Slang for dancing

for a man who had been a seaman nine years before. Newsweek wrote 'Steele is a delight of a kind that does not exist on the American stage. He is what every good entertainer must be – a direct giver of pleasure.' One writer referred to his 'natural talent and charisma.'[338] Another commented that Tommy 'projected a kind of wide-eyed innocent warmth across the footlights' noting that 'the show has been an absolute sell-out.' He went on 'he is a dedicated artiste, a thorough professional and a young man with a rare quality – a solidly ticking brain.'[339] A rare trait indeed. Another described him as a 'tow-headed, loose-legged cockney: so charming and gifted: one cannot estimate the heights to which he can climb.'[340] Tom claimed to lose five pounds every performance because he worked so hard.[341]

Within months of opening, Tommy was winner of the 1965 *Outer Critics Circle Award* for 'Outstanding Theatrical Achievement.' The OCC is the official organization of New York theatre writers for out-of-town newspapers and national publications and their awards are presented annually for theatrical achievements on and off Broadway. Further he won the Whitbread Anglo-American Theatre Award for Outstanding Performance in a Musical. He was nominated for a Tony Award[123] for Best Musical Actor in 1965. The show itself was nominated for a further eight Tonies.

Quite early on in the run, Tom (who had clearly been watched by Disney representatives) received an invitation to take luncheon with Walt Disney. He has

---

[123] Antoinette Perry Awards for Excellence in Broadway

often told the story of how he and his wife were picked up one Sunday morning and driven to an airport. From there he found himself on a plane from which he disembarked in California. Over lunch he was asked to star in the film *The Happiest Millionaire*. Having studied the script he told Disney that he did not like it: and declined to accept the offer. Astonished Disney executives asked him what the problem was. Tom told them that his part would need to be re-written. To *his* surprise a new script appeared several months later and he agreed to appear in the film. His relationship with Disney proved to be warm: and the two men found much in common in terms of wanting to provide wholesome family entertainment. It was a friendship which terminated very early with the death of Walt Disney a year later from lung cancer: Disney had always been a heavy smoker. 6th June saw Tommy appearing on the *Ed Sullivan Show* along with the cast of *Half a Sixpence* in which he and the cast sang *Let Me Sing A Happy Song* and *Money to Burn*.[342]

14th February 1966 he appeared with Gene Kelly in CBS's musical/dancing special *Gene Kelly in New York, New York*.[124] Kelly had seen Tom at the Broadhurst Theatre and visited him in his dressing room after the show. He invited Tommy to appear in a television show with him. Kelly said of Steele "He is the best export Britain has sent over here. All the superlatives that I have used in my life can be applied to him. He is a great performer and has a wonderful future ahead of him."[343] When you think about it: it does not get much better than

---

[124] A musical/dancing special featuring Gene Kelly and presenting New York City.

that. Tommy sang *Two of a Kind* with Kelly. It had actually been filmed in 1965: they rehearsed for three months and Tom always said that the experience nearly killed him. Woody Allen also danced in the show.[344]

28th March he appeared on Perry Como's *Kraft Music Hall*[125] singing both a vivacious *Little White Bull* (with the help of a bemused and confused American audience) *and* a duet with Liza Minnelli.

Tommy terminated his contract with Larry Parnes on the 6th Nov 1965 a historic event; for Parnes had been sole manager since 1961. Ian Bevan continued as his agent. At the same time news emerged that Paramount Pictures were going to film *Half a Sixpence*. On the same historic date, Tommy appeared on *Music from the Movies* presented by Desmond Carrington: it was one of a number of occasions that Carrington was to feature Tom's work over a period of fifty years.

Tristram Fane Saunders reports that Tommy Steele nearly beat Patrick Troughton to the lead role in *Doctor Who*. Anneke Wills who played the Doctor's companion Polly, said that Steele's name was put forward as a possible replacement for William Hartnell. "We all knew Bill[126] was going to leave at the end of the summer season," said Wills. "There were discussions: is that the end of the show *or* shall we have another actor? And then there were all the different people who were up for it: Michael Hordern was one, Tommy Steele was another

---

[125] Musical variety series sponsored by Kraft Foods.
[126] Hartnell

one, and I thought – coo, he's sexy. That would be good."³⁴⁵ It would have been a strange bit of casting.

19th March 1966 Tommy returned to London after leaving the New York production of *Half a Sixpence*: critics felt that without him the show had lost 'some of its charm and vitality.'³⁴⁶ He enjoyed five week's holiday before starting to film *The Happiest Millionaire* at Disney Studios on 5th May. It was to be the last live-action film[127] to be supervised personally by Walt Disney.³⁴⁷

Happiest Millionaire completed; Tommy returned to the UK in September 1966 to start shooting the film of *Half a Sixpence* on 19th September: filming took place at Eastbourne, Henley-on-Thames, Tunbridge Wells and Blenheim Palace among other locations.³⁴⁸ While filming at Blenheim Palace he not only met Senator Robert Kennedy but also took a break to support an appeal for funds by the St John Ambulance Brigade. He donated sixpence.³⁴⁹

27th October saw Tommy attend Alma Cogan's burial after her early death from ovarian cancer.[128] She and Tom were great mates and poker players: they appeared together several times (including as noted his television debut). She had also been particularly close to Lionel Bart.³⁵⁰ Digressing for a moment, Tommy had a fearsome reputation as a poker player: Cliff Michelmore teased him about it in his BBC interview *Personal Choice*

---

[127] Live action is a form of cinematography or videography that uses photography instead of animation
[128] In deference to family custom, her death was observed with traditional Jewish rites, with burial at the Jewish Cemetery in Bushey

on 4th February 1968. Tommy asked Michelmore who had told him and said teasingly "Was it Channing Pollock?"[129] Michelmore declined to tell him.

At this very time, and incredible though it seems, Tommy was celebrating his tenth anniversary in show business. There were to be many more similar celebrations in the years ahead. In an affectionate tribute Derek Johnson, writing in NME, described Tommy as one of the most successful and widely appealing family entertainers that England had ever produced.[351] He described him as a man with vast reserves of talent and personality and he considered that *Half a Sixpence* was the key to his acceptance as one of the world's great musical comedy stars. He continued, 'This country can be proud of him.' It was. Then on 14th November that year's *Royal Variety Performance* was staged. Alf Ramsey held the World Cup aloft on stage and Tommy appeared for the third time.

Sunday 20th November[130] Tom played on the right wing for a TV All Stars XI against a Welsh International XI at Ninian Park Cardiff to raise money for survivors of the Aberfan disaster[131] which had occurred nearby on the 21st October.[352] Richardson reports that it was a 7-7 draw in which Tommy scored and that after the match he was mobbed and knocked out. She says that police found him

---

[129] Pollock was recognized as one of the most sophisticated and charismatic magicians of his generation
[130] The first Sunday soccer match ever played in Wales
[131] The catastrophic collapse of a colliery spoil tip which killed 144 people: mostly children sitting in their classrooms

unconscious on the pitch and that a Dr Hamilton treated him for shock.[353] He was probably used to it by then.

On 15th January 1967 Tommy appeared in a special edition of BBC's *Movie Go Round* honouring Walt Disney. He was the right man to do it.

26th March Tommy played a major role in *The Heart of Show Business*: an important televised charity event put on to raise funds for victims and survivors of the Aberfan Disaster. Originally, a charity stage show was planned: seeming the best and most practical idea. Why not a television show? What about Elstree Studios?[354] Led by Welshman Harry Secombe, the response from stars of stage and screen had been incredible:

★ Elizabeth Taylor and Richard Burton flew in from Rome.
★ Sammy Davis Jr. stayed over specially after the *Royal Variety Performance.*
★ Shirley Bassey arrived from Las Vegas; saying she felt "she *ought* to be in the show."
★ Tommy Steele wanted to sing his number from the top of a Welsh mountain; until the production problems were pointed out to him.

Tommy sang *The King's New Clothes* with the Corona Children.[132]

---

[132] Rona Knight had opened the Corona Academy of Stage Training in Chiswick. In 1955, the Corona Academy moved to Hammersmith. The school supplied the young cast for Lionel Bart's *Oliver*. Tom worked with them on several occasions

The world première of the *Happiest Millionaire* was screened at Hollywood's Pantages Theatre on 23rd June 1967. The film was poorly received. The critics criticized its lengthy runtime. It proved to be a box office disappointment.[355] Mark Robinson unkindly described the film as a 'dud'[356] commenting: 'It is interesting to think what the final product would have looked like had Disney survived to infuse it with his special brand of magic. The final product is one of the biggest duds the studio ever churned out. That is not to say that it lacks little bursts of excellence.' Robinson did not think much of Tommy Steele either, about whom he commented: 'The most uncomfortable performance in the film is the ever-combustible Tommy Steele who overacts with such ferocity that it feels like he is in an entirely different picture altogether.' This was the type of criticism to be levelled at Tommy Steele several times later in his career. Interestingly, many years later, Susan King wrote in the Los Angeles Times that '*The Happiest Millionaire* is much better than what the critics declared thirty-two years ago.'[357] In spite of some of the critical comments at least Tommy was nominated for a Golden Globe Award in 1968 for *New Star of The Year – Actor.*

A Californian newspaper announced *Happiest Millionaire* as follows: 'Walt Disney has plucked a delightfully goofy cockney to star in a new movie in which he dances with a live and evil-tempered alligator. Steele resembles a great deal one of Disney's animated squirrels. But the kid has courage. His dance partner's sole aim in life is to nip off one of Tommy's twinkling toes or perhaps his entire leg.' It quoted Tommy: "If the dance sequence works it will be the most outstanding musical number in movie history. If not, people will be asking who's that idiot with the alligator." The paper continued: 'Tommy's accent is so strong sometimes It is impossible to comprehend what he is saying. But his cockney sense of humour is always in evidence. It is Steele's considered opinion that alligators are thoroughly untenable.' Tommy said: "To work with an alligator, you have got to be one of two things: out of work or out of your mind."[358]

The song *Fortuosity* was written for Tommy replacing a song called *Off Rittenhouse Square*:[133] a demo of which appeared on the re-issue of the film's CD soundtrack in 2002. As noted, the film was released after Walt Disney's death on 15th December - with his passing went the idea of Tommy making a whole series of family-oriented films for Disney. Too bad.

Farfetched though the story sounds, Tommy then found himself in *Finian's Rainbow* playing the Irish leprechaun Og. Some years ago, Tommy related that he went to lunch at the BBC studios in London and was asked to appear in the forthcoming Warner Brothers/Seven Arts film of *Finian's Rainbow*. He questioned why Warner Brothers wanted him. His story is that the reply was "Because you are Irish" (because he had played the part of an Irish butler in the *Happiest Millionaire*).

One of his most oft repeated stories originates from this production. He turned up at the studios and was

---

[133] Which is a public park in Pittsburgh

introduced to co-star Fred Astaire[134] who promptly told him that his method of tap dancing was all wrong. The fault, Astaire suggested, was that Gene Kelly had taught him to dance. Be that as it may, Tommy Steele must be the only major star in history to have learned tap dancing with both Kelly and Astaire. He clearly had a warm relationship with the former.

Production commenced in Hollywood on 25th June 1967. It was the first major film directed by Francis Ford Coppola and was eventually released on 9th October 1968. UPI reported that on 9th August Petula Clark and Tommy pre-recorded songs for *Finian's Rainbow* before cameras began rolling on the film.[359] At the conclusion of filming, Fred Astaire hosted one of the largest and best-attended set parties in studio history: it featured three bars and entertainment from an orchestra. Over four hundred guests, including members of the cast and crew and their spouses, attended the picture wind-up bash:[360] just another Hollywood extravaganza.

Amusingly it was announced that a musical based on the life of Dr Barnardo was planned called *Please Sir*: and that it would star Tommy Steele: he promptly announced that it would not. In the BBC's *Disney Time* on 28th August Tommy introduced some of the heroes and villains - both live and in cartoons - who had appeared in Walt Disney films. It included scenes from *Peter Pan, Treasure Island, The Million Dollar Collar, Three Little Pigs, Robin Hood, Jungle Book* and *The Happiest Millionaire*.

---

[134] Whose last musical it was

The film version of *Half a Sixpence* opened in London on 21st December at the West End Astoria and was nominated for one BAFTA film award. It was the first Hollywood movie to be shot entirely in the UK.[361] Roger Ebert commented 'Tommy Steele is just the performer for this sort of schmaltz. He is, in fact, a very good song-and-dance man, the only member of his generation who bears comparison with Gene Kelly and Dan Dailey.'[135/362] Praise indeed. Other reviewers commented on his natural talent and charisma: his having given a dazzling, perfected performance; *and* the broad brash ebullience of Tommy Steele.[363]

As noted earlier, 4th February 1968 Tommy was interviewed by Cliff Michelmore on BBC's *Personal Choice*.[136] Michelmore had known and admired Tommy Steele for some years and was delighted to see him established as an international star. He wanted to know how this success had come about and why Tom had succeeded where so many others had failed. He said "I think it is not only talent, I think it is because of his refreshingly open honesty."[364] Incidentally, Michelmore had tackled the famous Kennedy and Parnes on the BBC's *Tonight* programme[137] over the matter of their working the young Tommy Steele to the bone. Tommy's mother had written to Michelmore about this on 7th May 1958: she was fed up with it.[365] Michelmore had received a letter of thanks from Mrs Hicks for confronting the pair.[366]

---

[135] American dancer and actor
[136] Well-known interviewers chose the people they wished to interview
[137] Popular current affairs programme at the time

4th March Tommy Steele appeared at the Royal Film Performance of *Romeo and Juliet* at the Odeon Leicester Square.

As noted, *Finian's Rainbow* premièred in October (9th in the US, 10th in London). Yet again Tommy was accused of over-acting and it was suggested that his mugging spoiled the likes of *When I'm Not Near the Girl I Love*.[367] However, Roger Ebert was kinder. He wrote that 'the film gave you that same wonderful sense you got from any of the great musicals: that it knows exactly where it is going and is getting there as quickly, and with as much fun, as possible.' He continued, 'it is also enchanting and that's a word I don't get to use much. Tommy Steele, as always, is a shade overdone, but perhaps a leprechaun should be a shade overdone.'[368] NME added that 'it was Tommy's usual loveable, likeable, impish act as Og.'

In Miami, Tommy was awarded the *Star of the Future* award from America's top movie theatres owners. It was presented to him at the National Association of Theatre Owners of America's annual convention.[369]

CHAPTER FIVE

BACK TO THE CLASSICS

After three years of non-stop studio work, Tommy signed to play Feste in *Twelfth Night* to be featured in ITV's *Sunday Night Theatre* which was to be filmed in early 1968. It was two years before it would be shown on television on 12th July 1970. His casting was described as 'unlikely but surprisingly effective:' a 'Shakespearian newcomer, Cockney entertainer Tommy Steele as Feste, complete with songs.'[370]

A distinguished and highly experienced casting played alongside the singer-turned-actor Tommy Steele: they included Shakespearean performers Joan Plowright, Ralph Richardson and Alec Guinness. Although a long-term fan,[138] Tommy had never acted in Shakespeare before. He gave a perfectly competent performance but his Feste was a good deal younger and sunnier of disposition than one would normally expect.[371]

Conrad Brunstrom shared the general mood writing that Tommy smiled a lot: in fact, at the height of his fame in the 1960s he was always grinning. The Tommy Steele smile was not quite an André Rieu[139] slappable smile, but a smile you think about slapping before allowing your arm to flop down to your thigh. He

---
[138] Tommy claimed to have seen the 1955 film directed by Laurence Olivier of Richard III twenty times
[139] A Dutch conductor

continued 'I do think Tommy Steele smiles too much for Feste. Tommy Steele is more of a Will Kempe clown than a Robert Armin clown and in many ways, Feste is a nasty piece of work. The whirligig of time brings in his revenges with a look of cold-blooded satisfaction. Not with the grin of Tommy Steele.'[372]

At least the British Theatre Guide understood. It said 'this was a beautifully spoken production which did not prevent Tommy Steele playing Feste from twinkling as only he can and singing at every opportunity.'[373] The critics rarely appreciated Tommy playing a role as a cheerful, happy man. Perhaps an element of it was that Tommy described himself as a "A bit of a show off; I was always trying to get into the limelight at school."[374] This might explain the incessant grin - and his trait of over dramatization was probably misunderstood by serious critics.

9th March Tommy signed to play Jack Shepherd in *Where's Jack*: the title theme was to be whistled by Roger Whittaker.[140] The film related the exploits of a notorious 18th-century thief and prison-breaker. The film was shot in County Wicklow reaffirming the notion of those who believed that the cockney sprite was in fact an Irish Leprechaun. The film was released on April Fool's Day 1969. Mark Cunliffe summed it up well 'the titular role of Jack went to none other than Tommy Steele who, a decade earlier, was Britain's first rock 'n' roll teen idol but had developed his career into that of a song and dance man. It was a bold and unusual choice as Sheppard was, after all, only twenty-one at the height of his criminal

---

[140] Issued as a B side on a single on Philips

fame and the screenplay had the then thirty-three-year-old Steele state his age as twenty or thereabouts. Nevertheless, it worked. Steele's physique matched the lightly built, diminutive rogue. He was one of the first cockney pop stars to play a criminal:'[375] but, you see, he was a good actor.

Tommy returned to the British stage for the first time since 1965 (when he ended his triumphant appearance in *Half a Sixpence*) opening at the New Oxford Theatre on 26th November 1968 in *The Servant of Two Masters*. It was a new production directed by Toby Robertson. While there a famous sketch – a caricature – of Tommy as Truffaldino was drawn by Gilbert Sommerlad a rehearsal pianist and orchestral violinist at the Oxford New Theatre. Sommerlad sketched the stars on stage while he was not needed in the orchestra pit and stored the sketches in a series of albums.[376] The production was a new English translation ('a brilliant adaptation')[141] by David Turner and Paul Lapworth and was first staged with Tommy in the main role. Reviews, as usual, were mixed. Michael Billington said it was 'As English as boiled beef and carrots' while suggesting that 'Tommy essayed[142] the part with an obvious desire to do an ingratiating star-turn.'[377] The Spectator was kinder remarking that he played Truffaldino with 'an adroit cockney breeziness:' which, of course, was the essence of the man himself. The Sun commented that Tommy 'has that indefinable thing called stage presence, He performs

---

[141] https://www.stageplays.com/products/the_servant_of_two_masters1

[142] Old fashioned – 'to try to do something'

with grace and skill'[378] while the Sketch said 'Tommy Steele has the touch. His timing is excellent and he has a tremendous talent for the live theatre.'[379] The trouble, with which so many critics grappled over the years, was that Tommy simply could not help being the man that he is. 'You are what you are' and that, at the end of the day, has always been his greatest strength. The show went on to the Wimbledon Theatre (2nd December), the Theatre Royal Brighton (9th) and the Queen's Theatre, London (18th). While at Brighton, Sir Laurence Olivier came to see the play and said to Tommy – with regard to his performance – "The problem is you don't love the character."[380]

It might be argued that this era was the most creative of Tommy's professional life. For a period of a perhaps a dozen years, a whole stream of highly successful and different forms of communication streamed from him. First, was *Tommy Steele and Things*. It was shown by the BBC on *Omnibus* on the 21st December 1969 the BBC described it as 'An uncomplicated film by a happy man.'[381] This is a description that many of his critics might have born in mind over the years as, this writer believes, he never set out to be anything other than that. Richardson quotes Sean Day Lewis writing that 'this journey through memories would have offended nobody.' He continued, 'Tommy showed himself as he would wish to be seen as happy and uncomplicated. The cameraman provided the liveliest visual view of London that I have seen for a long time. Childhood in Bermondsey cannot have been much fun.

Mr Steele is a very likeable personality and has made a very likeable film.'[382] It was a tribute handsomely paid.

Tommy Steele and Things was a musical film written and performed by the star himself telling something of his own background in and around Bermondsey; an area and its people of which he was rightly very proud (and where he always felt that he belonged). The camera moved through his native Bermondsey looking at people and places which meant so much to him. He visited the now derelict Troc-Ette cinema[143] to which he went as a child; he ate in the local Pie and Mash shop; and took a morning plunge in the Public Baths. The film was produced by John Gibson who died in 1974 at the age of 49. Years later Tommy described Gibson as a wonderful man who was always drunk: and he said that working with him was the happiest experience of his professional life. Tommy visited Bacon School in Pages Walk (where he was a pupil from 1946 to 1951 and for whom he had become its most famous old boy) and where some filming had been done. He showed the film to the students and explained what it was all about.

On The Times website there is a section called *We've got mail - the greatest letters sent to The Times.* Tom's letter dated 8th February 1969 is headlined. It read:[144]

---

[143] Now the site of Troc-Ette mansions – the theatre was a casualty of the popularity of television and was closed in January 1956

[144] Subsequent to Tommy reading an article about the lamentable demise of Tony Hancock

Sir,

I feel that perhaps a little more could be said concerning the profession, the environment, the very existence of a comedian. The big difference between a dramatic actor and a comedian is basically one of 'sound.' They both thrive in creating emotions in their audience, but it is the lot of the comedian also to create a sound - laughter. It is not enough for him to feel the moment is amusing, he must hear the audience feel it. This can, and quite often does, cause deep anxiety to the man whose task it is to make an audience forget their anxieties. He dreads the day his timing goes; he fears his audience; he thrives on laughs and dies with silence. It is said that when the end of a comedian is at hand, he "dies from the eyes." Sit in an audience long enough and you have to see it at least once in your life. He stares transfixed. You will feel his animosity with every line. He loved you once, but now you frighten him. He knows you will never laugh for him again. Such a comedian is not unlike Manolete.[145] He is tortured into risking all to please his audience and, alas, as in the case of the great Tony Hancock, he comes to the same end for the same reason.

Yours,

TOMMY STEELE

---

[145] The celebrated bullfighter

~~~ it was in this letter that Tommy Steele approached greatness for the first time.

27th March the long-awaited Miss Emma Hicks was born.

Meanwhile, in another busy year, he had moved to Montrose House, Petersham, where he lived for over thirty years. Afterwards he moved to an exclusive eight floor Thames-side apartment (formerly Alembic House) commanding spectacular views across the river towards Westminster: Lord Archer owns the penthouse above him.

Montrose House, Petersham, is on a sharp corner, which locals referred to as *the Tommy Steele Corner*. This writer has travelled past the house on a bus on many occasions. A life-size statue of Charlie Chaplin as *The Tramp* stood outside Steele's home.

Tommy also owned a Mobile garage on Petersham Road together with the neighbouring Pot Shop. He is reported as saying that he purchased the petrol station to prevent a skyscraper being built there: legend has it that he himself served petrol there occasionally:[383] one can certainly believe it. He sold the house for £6.5m in 2004.[384] One of the features of this great house was a squash court. As he owned it, Tommy decided to use it: as one does. He developed a love of the sport, rapidly becoming very good at it. Eventually he represented Surrey. In his mémoires, the late disgraced publicist Max Clifford tells how he was introduced to squash by Tommy Steele through mutual friend Lennie Bennett (who he described as a 'terrific player').[385] A sign of Tom's prowess is that on 20th May 1978 he teamed up with Mohibullah Khan to play

Leonard Rossiter and Hiuddy Jahan in the Pro-Celebrity Squash Rank Xerox Challenge Final.

12th July NME reported that Tommy was to star in the stage musical *Piccadilly*: of which this writer believes no more was ever heard. A month later on 8th August it was announced – this time correctly – that Tommy was to star that Christmas in a new pantomime at the London Palladium – *Dick Whittington* – and that he would play the lead role. Although he had appeared there in *Sunday Night at the London Palladium* and in the *Royal Variety Performance* this would be his first appearance there in pantomime. Needless to say, the producers had engaged a cat to play Whittington's famous feline and, in the course of a publicity stunt, the cat broke free and was photographed being chased by Tom into the grounds of nearby Whittington Hospital on Magdala Avenue. In another stunt, Tom rode in the Lord Mayor's procession on 13th November.[386] The pantomime opened on 23rd December and ran for three months.

Richardson aptly quoted Tommy "Who wants to go to a panto in April? Even the Box Office Manager cannot believe it. It is standing room only. I think that the public are looking for wholesome entertainment. There is an old Music Hall gag that if you cannot get any laughs - trying letting your trousers down. If it ever comes to that, mate, I would rather go out of business."[387]

Meanwhile on the 27th December, and for the second time, Tommy Steele broadcast as the guest on *Desert Island Discs* nominating the gramophone records he would take to a desert island: and, as a luxury good, a sports car: which might make sense as one supposes that he would not get speeding tickets on a desert island.

It was now eleven years since Cinderella; Tommy Steele swept back onto the London stage in a follow up pantomime. The Palladium was to become the venue which he was to make his own. The show was also, of course, his first appearance with Mary Hopkin with whom he later performed in a summer show at Blackpool. This writer has two particular memories of the production of Dick Whittington. One a lovely cat: and the other the star sweeping onto the centre of the stage singing *Fortuosity*[146] as the opening number. Leslie A. MacDonnell wrote in the programme, for what was to be his final pantomime as Managing Director of Moss Empires: 'all records would be broken'. He described the production as 'the greatest and most spectacular in the history of the London Palladium.' We wonder what he would have written about *Singin' in the Rain* just over a decade later. Demand was so great that the run was extended for an additional month. The programme concluded that Tommy's golden touch had enabled him to succeed in every entertainment medium with which he had been involved. So, it proved again in this production of *Dick Whittington*.

An all star-studded cast, led by Tommy Steele, once again broke all the records at the world's most famous theatre: as, indeed, Tommy Steele was to achieve again and again. Sir Harold Hobson[147] wrote: 'children who saw the show would tell their children's children that

---

[146] From the *Happiest Millionaire*
[147] The Sunday Times

they had witnessed Tommy Steele in all his pantomime glory.'[148] It was a triumph for him and a wonderful show. The Daily Telegraph noticed 'the zest brought to the show by Tommy Steele and his *life of the party* ebullience: he exploits a quite special charm.'[388]

The summer of 1970 saw Tom reunited with Mary Hopkin (an unlikely pairing?) for *The Tommy Steele Show* which ran at the ABC Blackpool[149] from 11th July for eleven weeks. This might be classed as a seminal event. It was an opportunity for him to hone his skills as the one man in a one-man show - which he was to take to Las Vegas early the following year. He sang *Mississippi Riverboat* and Irish laments: and a pigeon sat on his head ~ as Patrick O'Neill suggested, it was impressed by the master in action.[389]

Before, and after his summer season in Blackpool, Tommy was working on a second documentary for the BBC *Omnibus* programme; this was filmed in late 1970. The result was *Tommy Steele in search of Charlie Chaplin*. Broadcast on 12th April 1971 - again produced by John Gibson - this was a historical and sentimental musical journey. Once again filmed in Bermondsey from which area both Chaplin and Steele came: Tommy was stepping back in time to a London of the early 1900s: exploring the poverty and the hilarity that influenced the boy who would become the greatest clown in the world.

---

[148] This writer thought that this was the greatest compliment ever paid to Tommy Steele

[149] Fairly new – it had been opened by the mayor of Blackpool seven years before

Tommy was photographed leaving Heathrow Airport on 13th February with a troop of dancers bound for Las Vegas: they were Michele Hardy, Dawn MacDonald, Connie Reid and Shereen Penders.[390]

18th February saw Tommy appearing at Caesar's Palace in Las Vegas at the start of a three-week engagement. Caesar's Palace claimed this to be his world cabaret debut. That it was not: that had taken place at the Café de Paris in January 1957 and had been his first gigantic triumph. He received a standing ovation from a star-studded audience. Beat Magazine quoted The Hollywood Reporter: 'He has the charm and versatility of a young Danny Kaye. He is a marvellous one-man show.'[391] Forrest Duke described him as the 'nightclub find of the decade:' another reporter commented 'England's own Tommy Steele is on a par with Al Johnson and Maurice Chevalier.'[392]

Following what proved to be an enormous success in Las Vegas, the ubiquitous Harold Fielding said to Tommy: "Let's take this show to London." So, it came about that on 7th April Tom found himself at the Adelphi Theatre on the Strand (from where Fielding had taken off *Charlie Girl*) in *Meet me in London* for a ten-week season.

Next Tom returned to his happy stamping ground in Scandinavia where he appeared in Copenhagen at the Tivoli Gardens in July, at Bern's[150] Stockholm being greeted with wild acclaim just as he had been as a rock 'n' roll singer a decade before and at the Chat Noir theatre[151]

---

[150] Nightclub at Berns Hotel

in Oslo.³⁹³ He then proceeded to the Coventry Theatre where he opened on 6th October for a seven week season starring in the *1971 Birthday Show*.¹⁵² He continued to develop the one-man show on which he had started work at Blackpool the year before. The programme notes at Coventry refer to his great personal triumph in Las Vegas. It is interesting to reflect that when it was announced that he was going to Las Vegas, Billboard said that he had contracted to appear there several years in succession for six weeks at a time: yet he never returned.³⁹⁴ Never believe what you read in the papers.

1972 must have seemed quite restful to Tommy Steele. But before that rest, he appeared at Tivoli Gardens Concert Hall in Copenhagen on 1st January. Meanwhile, there had been much criticism of raucous chanting whilst *Abide with Me* was being sung before the kick off at the annual FA Cup Final. Someone had the inspired idea of asking Tommy Steele - a self-confessed football fanatic - to sing the hymn on 6th May to lead the vocals of the 100,000 crowd. It must have been quite a challenge for him. Needless to say – and wearing a very cool white suit - he carried it off with great aplomb. Subsequently, he spent much time working on two television projects. The first *The Tommy Steele Hour* was broadcast on London Weekend ITV on 14th May.

Billboard reported that Tommy was scheduled for a two-week season at Berns Night Club Stockholm in September.¹⁵³/³⁹⁵ Before the year ended, Tommy had

---

¹⁵¹ Black Cat
¹⁵² He had appeared in the 1961 Show ten years before
¹⁵³ Berns Hotel nightclub is a popular venue among serious

written and recorded *A Special Tommy Steele* his second major television show of the year. It was widely acclaimed and Britain's entry at that year's Montreux Festival. It was broadcast on LWT on the 20th January 1973. The programme opened with Tommy walking through a television studio singing a medley of songs from *Gypsy*. This was followed by a selection of songs from *Company*. The theme running through the show was *imagination* which had become an almost messianic theme with him. At the year end, on 29th December, the BBC broadcast *I wanna be an all-round entertainer:* an affectionate tribute presented by Frank Dixon.

By 12th March he was making a sentimental return to the O'Keefe Centre in Toronto where eight years before to the week he had trialled *Half a Sixpence* before its opening on Broadway. On what was to be his last appearance in Canada he opened his *London Palladium Show* (which was reprising his Las Vegas triumph of two years before). Unusually a first half turn was the popular British entertainer Dickie Henderson.[154] One member of the audience wrote: 'I acquired tickets for the last night of his week-long stand. I remember a packed house and a rapturous reception. And there was the Don Quixote routine where, suitably attired and mounted on a fake horse, he galloped round the stage in front of a filmed backdrop of English country roads. It was both clever and funny; the audience lapped it up.'[396]

Stockholm music fans: where they listen to live music presented by international artistes in an intimate and acoustically rich setting
[154] Popular British light entertainer in the '50s and '60s

Tom sailed back to the UK and prepared to open on 11th April at the London Palladium for six weeks with the *Tommy Steele Show*. This was to be another reincarnation of his Las Vegas act. Jack Tinker reported that he was 'warm, ebullient, matey and confiding: but never less than a star.' He reported that the show 'has a slick, glittering but unpretentious setting. He has an obvious delight in entertaining: and with impeccable professionalism.'[397]

At the same time two LPs were issued – *The Happy World of Tommy Steele* – which were the first of many regurgitations of his early Decca hits.

During 1973 Tommy was engaged to voice the title role in Disney's animated movie *Robin Hood* but it did not work out and he was replaced by Brian Bedford.[398]

Few people remember one extraordinary broadcast with which Tommy was associated. Shown on 19th August[399] Tommy appeared[155] as Buttons in the Granada production of *Once Upon a Time*.[156] One person who saw it described it thus: 'Cinderella and Prince Charming have just got married. Buttons has to flee for his life as he knows too much about Cinderella's past. He arrives in Paris in 1789 and becomes one of Robespierre's henchmen; but he lives in hope that Cinders will find out that the Prince's goons have been sent after him and insist he is pardoned. When he discovered that it was Cinders herself who sent the thugs, he persuades Robespierre that the Land of Charming is a part of France and the benefits

---

[155] Along with Peggy Mount
[156] Sometimes referred to simply as *Buttons*

of the Revolution must be taken to the people. At the end Buttons, who has by now adopted all Robespierre's dress and mannerisms, is leading the invasion force, taking a guillotine with him.' This extraordinary programme was performed in pantomime style, with overacting and addresses direct to the audience.'[400] Tommy and Alun Owen wrote the script: in one scene - and most unlike his public persona – Tommy was involved in a bedroom romp.

His experience in Las Vegas – and later at the Adelphi Theatre – had opened new horizons for Tommy. One was working in cabaret in nightclubs: which proved to be lucrative. He was the first person to appear on the stage[401] of the Dudley Hippodrome Casino Club which, having been taken over by Ladbrokes, became Cesar's (sic) Palace on 15th October:[402] he appeared on the opening night.

This led to a two-week stint in *The Tommy Steele Spectacular* in January 1974 at the Wakefield Theatre Club: negotiations were said to have taken several months. He was supported by eight dancers and a thirty-piece orchestra. The amount of his fee was not made public. It was said that few clubs could afford him or cope with the 'detailed technical conditions' on which he insisted. It was reported that the owner spent £10,000 on alterations and equipment. One commentator said that he launched into the most polished hour of all-in entertainment that one was likely to see for a long time.[403]

Tommy Taylor was a compère and worked at the Wakefield Theatre Club. He suffered from stage fright and discussed this with the owner. He in turn related to him that Tommy Steele got so nervous that he could be physically ill on his way to the stage.[404] This was born out later in a discussion that Tommy had with Michael Parkinson in 1979. He told the audience that he always suffered from nerves before a show and was often physically sick.[405]

Whilst he was in Scandinavia in September for his cabaret and concert tour, Tommy conceived the idea of writing his musical memoires. Now in 1930, Christina Foyle (an optimistic, free-thinker and heiress to what was then the world's largest bookstore) had decided that London was ready to digest a series of literary luncheons. They became a national institution and were much discussed by the chattering classes. On September the 9th 1974, Tommy Steele made history as the first ever recorded guest (if you will excuse the pun) invited to launch his musical autobiography.

The previous April had found Tommy at Pye Recording Studios at Great Cumberland Place making an LP *My Life, My Song*. This was issued in a gatefold album with an illustrated lyric book inside. This LP was the subject of the Foyle's luncheon. Supporting the promotion of the same work, on 8th October the BBC broadcast Episode 27, Season 8 of *Omnibus*: *Tommy Steele: My Life, My Song*. In this broadcast Tommy performed a concert featuring self-written auto-biographical songs; followed by an interview with Melvyn Bragg.

In a sense one might describe this as his life's work. It was one of the world's few musical autobiographies and was handsomely published. The gatefold LP featured twelve of his own paintings: some of which were later issued as prints. Several of these are now collectors' items in their own right and some are much sought after: indeed, they established his name as a painter of some merit. Tom obviously got much satisfaction from the production of this work for he continued to use some of the numbers in his one-man show for many years afterwards. It was said that 'he paints with a verve and simplicity which is typical both of him personally and as a performer. He has a great feeling for colour.'[406] The then Bishop of Bath and Wells once remarked to the author: "I am in the business of communication." Too true. At an early stage, Tommy Steele perceived that he was a 'communicator' and that sculpture, painting and writing were all forms of the genre. Steele's talents as a showman *and communicator* have been crucial to his success.[407]

CHAPTER SIX

ANOTHER GOLDEN YEAR

October 1974 saw a one-man exhibition of Tommy's paintings at the Christopher Wade Gallery in London: had they been for sale it would have been a sell-out.[408] It was also featured on Nationwide.[157]

And then, as you might say, came a flash and a bang. For 17th December Tommy opened at the London Palladium in *Hans Andersen*. A musical in two acts by Tommy Steele and Beverley Cross. Based on the 1952 film *Hans Christian Andersen*, the lyrics and music were taken from the film score and other works by Frank Loesser. This writer always felt that it was Tommy Steele's finest – and definitive – work. *Hans Andersen* was supposed to run at the London Palladium for the 1974-75 Christmas season. However, box office reaction was enormous and it ran for almost a year, notching up 383 performances closing on 1st November 1975.

It is said that the days immediately preceding the opening night were fraught with tension. At one point, Tommy threatened to walk out unless a specific series of changes were made and there was also a tempestuous disagreement with musical director Alyn Ainsworth. But

---
[157] Popular BBC television news and current affairs programme

things were sorted by the night itself and a standing ovation ensued.[409]

In 1975 the Post Office[158] hired Tommy to give his stamp of approval both to the campaign to send letters *and* to post early for Christmas. To what extent the campaign was worthwhile has never been disclosed.

10th October was a day of great excitement in Rotherhithe - one attracting national attention - because Tommy Steele unveiled a statue sculpted in honour of his father (the first Bermondsey boy that he had known), Tommy Hicks Senior.[159] It was located at Rotherhithe Civic Centre by the Library on Albion Street.[160] The statue was a self-portrait, representing Tommy as a boy, head down and moving headlong into the future carrying a book under his arm. Alas, bovver boys set fire to the statue in 1998: its remains disappeared and have never been found or replaced. If you visit the location today and ask after it few people have any idea what you are talking about.

July 1976 saw a drama in the Steele household. The entertainer turned up at Battersea Dogs' Home accompanied by his distraught seven-year-old daughter. The family's much-loved Yorkshire Terrier, Tramp, had disappeared from their home three days earlier. They had come to the Home as a last resort. Within minutes they were reunited with their pet, which had been collected and brought in by Richmond Police two days earlier. "He is

---

[158] As it was then constituted: now Royal Mail Group
[159] Known to his family as Darbo
[160] Both of which are now closed

only a tatty scruff. We call him *Tramp* because he always looks as though he needs a wash," Tommy told reporters afterwards, "Emma imagined he had been kidnapped or run over,"[410] as one would.

Hans Andersen was a mega success. It left London after fifteen months and commenced a semi-national tour: starting in Manchester on 15th December (for nine weeks), Birmingham 21st February (four weeks) and the Hippodrome Bristol on 27th March 1976 (four weeks). Richardson recalls that Tom flew into Manchester with Harold Fielding and Louis Benjamin on an executive jet to publicize the run - and in doing so split his trousers.[411] We have all done it. She notes that the show was Manchester's biggest ever box office advance. A reviewer commented on his 'teeth flashing and corn hair bobbing.' Jack Good was struck by his twinkling eyes and wonderful shining teeth.[412] Those teeth again: you really felt that by now reviewers had truly got their teeth into it and that perhaps they might have had something more substantive to write about.

Whilst appearing in Manchester, Tommy called upon the great painter L. S. Lowry. Tommy had performed with fifty dancers in a routine called *Same Size Boots* in which the dance routine brought a Lowry painting to life. He took a video (together with a video recorder) of the dance routine and played it to Lowry. The artist said "It's wonderful." Tommy said "Would you like to see it again?" Lowry said "Would they mind?"[413]

1976 was to prove to be another golden year (although this time without the celebratory television programme). The autumn saw the twentieth anniversary of Tom's meteoric rise to fame. It was marked by the 1956-1976 *Seven-City Anniversary Show*: the cast included Lennie Bennett[161] for the first time. He went on to become a good friend and fellow squash player. Tommy was in Coventry on 6th September promoting the show.[414] It opened on 12th October at the Coventry Theatre: then continued on to 19th, Theatre Royal Nottingham, 26th Gaumont Theatre Southampton, 2nd November Grand Theatre and Opera House Leeds, 9th Aberdeen, 16th Sunderland Empire and 23rd Palace Theatre Manchester.

Richard Mills[162] recalls that to celebrate the twentieth anniversary of Tommy's entry into show business he suggested that he should do an Anniversary show for the Autumn Season at Coventry. Mills recalls that Tommy was loath to do this: but he said that he would agree, provided he was paid a salary which left him enough money after tax to buy a particular painting of which he was particularly fond.

Mills remembers asking him if he would like to have a party after the opening night. Tommy replied "Let's have a meal at the restaurant at the nearby Leofric Hotel.[163] You have your table with your friends and nearby I'll have a table with my family. If the show works - we'll join up: but you pick up the bill."

---

[161] Northern comedian
[162] Then Chief Executive of Bernard Delfont Ltd
[163] Now student flats

Mills continued: "The show was a success, and we joined up. Tommy as usual had his favourite food which was lobster. When I received the bill at the end of the evening, Tommy said, I hope you don't mind my asking, but how much did they charge for the lobster? Seventy-nine pounds," I replied. "That's absolutely outrageous" he said. "Pay the bill, but do not pay for the lobster." He arranged for his Personal Assistant to get up at 3.00 a.m. the next morning, drive to a fishing village and buy a lobster. His P.A. arrived back with it. Tommy wrapped it up with half a pound of butter and sent it to the Manager of the Leofric Hotel, in lieu of payment. Mills writes "We never heard another word."[415]

Spring 1977 he recorded *Tommy Steele and a Show* for Thames Television (which was broadcast later on 28th September). On 4th July he talked with Pete Murray on *Open House* on BBC 2.

The Festival Theatre in Paignton was opened in 1967 and enjoyed a very short lifespan before being changed into a cinema in 1999. During its short life Tommy was one of the major celebrities to appear there: starring in the *Summer Show* in 1977 opening on 5th August. The performance was recorded during its run and the resulting LP was on sale when Tom appeared in theatres for years afterwards. It is still worth listening to today to get a feel for the glories of his one-man show and how he engaged with his audience. On the LP he much enjoys talking to a group of women from Plymouth who were in the audience. Richard Mills again had to persuade Tommy to appear. He writes: 'When I first approached Tommy to do the show, he was loath, but after I showed him the theatre, he reluctantly decided to do it. He said that part of his reason for not wanting to do Paignton was that he did not wish to be separated from his family for the whole of the summer. However, a very good nearby hotel provided him with an excellent suite of rooms. He moved Annie and Emma down to stay with him for the season. The hotel even provided a pet rabbit for Emma, which she kept on a flat roof just outside the windows of their suite. Everyone had a good time; Tommy as usual was sensational; and we totally sold out.'[416]

Not long after, in October 1977, he appeared at Jollees (where beer was on sale for 34p a pint) in the *Tommy Steele Spectacular*. Jollees was a live music and cabaret venue in Longton[164] and was at the time the largest capacity cabaret venue in the UK. 17th December Tom was back over Christmas at his beloved London Palladium for a reprise season of *Hans Andersen* with changes both to the cast and to the score. This time the production was directed by Tommy. This writer believes that a director needs to be independent of the star of the show: and that this was not a step forward.

The period 17th July 1978 through 12th August - and on the occasion of the 800th anniversary of the Tower of London - witnessed one of Tommy's greatest achievements. He was invited once again to participate in the *Festival of the City of London*. This time playing Jack Point in Gilbert and Sullivan's masterpiece the *Yeomen of the Guard*. Before the production he underwent training in

---

[164] One of six towns which amalgamated to form the county borough of Stoke-on-Trent

the specific art of opera singing. The operetta was filmed and shown on television on 23rd December.

Chris Webster[417] suggests that the version shown on television was not the actual performance at the Tower. He says 'the website states that Tommy Steele's *Yeoman* was videoed in various places at the Tower, but this is completely incorrect - at least it is for the video that I've just watched which is definitely a studio video recording, but adapted from the Anthony Besch City of London production. It is not an actual video of that production in situ.'

The tradition of staging *Yeomen of the Guards* at the Tower seems to have begun with the *Festival of Britain* in 1951. Performances took place on a stage erected across the moat outside the Tower.[418] As a precursor to the run, Tommy pretended to be decapitated at the Tower on the 5th April by two Yeomen Warders; it was photographed and much enjoyed by Evening Standard readers.[419]

The autumn saw a reprise of the *Tommy Steele Spectacular* at The Golden Garter[165] in Wythenshawe[166] on 16th October *and* The Wakefield Theatre Club. It was said that his act was the most lavish ever staged at the Garter.[420]

1979 got off to a good start. Tommy received the OBE in the New Year's Honours List (and it is shameful that public honours ended there until late 2020). Tom's

---

[165] 'The Garter', as it was affectionately known locally. It closed for ever in 1982
[166] A suburb south of Manchester

rich creative phase continued into 1979 with the release of *Tommy Steele's Family Album:* what else could it be called: it might have been the best LP that he ever released.

Readers will recall that 1962 saw an ATV television show entitled *Quincy's Quest.* Between December 1978 – March 1979 Tommy rehearsed for a new filmed version of *Quincy's Quest* for Thames Television. It was to be broadcast over Christmas 1979. It used a lot of cutting-edge camera and vision mixer trick effects of the day.[421] It was reported that it was the single most expensive television programme ever made in Britain: it was written, acted and staged by Tommy Steele:[422] he also co-composed the music. It was published in book form as *Quincy* by Mammoth in 1981.

This was a revised - and now more sophisticated - production. Tim Worthington wrote about it. He said: 'Quincy's Quest is one of those television shows that large numbers of people seem to remember for no readily obvious reason. Shown by ITV on 20th December, it was unquestionably one of the network's seasonal big guns at the end of a strike-stricken year during which the channel had lost a great deal of goodwill. It was plugged on the front cover of that week's TV Times: together with a massive boxout[167] taking up approximately eighty three percent of the day's listings. It is fair to say that ITV expected a few people to watch it. What they probably did not expect, however, was that it would make such an

---

[167] Text written to accompany a larger text and printed in a separate area of a page.

indelible impression on so many of those who did. At a time when most television was still considered ephemeral and throwaway, ITV's Light Entertainment output was considered even more ephemeral and throwaway still; especially so at Christmas. Yet *Quincy's Quest* seems to have burned itself into the memories of many viewers. Doubtless part of the reason for its success was that Tommy had obviously taken quite some time to perfect the production: as the earlier, shorter version had appeared on ITV as part of *The Tommy Steele Show* in December 1962. In all probability, his additional experience in big brash audience-friendly razzle-dazzle helped to give the 1979 version of *Quincy's Quest* its extra youngster-entrancing advantage.'423

Richard Mills relates that at Tommy Steele's New Year party they hatched a plan to do his one-man show at the Prince of Wales Theatre. Tommy would only do it on condition that it was tried out at Blackpool first. So, Tom prepared for *An Evening with Tommy Steele* at the ABC Blackpool. It ran from the 30th July until the 14th September: twice nightly: without an interval - read that carefully.

Mills recalls that it *did* work in Blackpool and that after the opening date for London had been set, Tommy said to him "Do you want the greatest piece of publicity that you have ever had for a show? If you do; give me £2,000." "What's it for?" Mills enquired. Tommy replied "I'm going to build a ten-foot-high statue of Charlie Chaplin in my hotel suite. Nobody will know, said Tommy. "How will you do that without anybody finding out?" Mills asked. "Don't worry, leave it with me"

Tommy responded. The whole shenanigans were all done in the greatest secrecy - even the transportation of it from the hotel to a kiln in Blackburn where it was fired.

Tommy had the statue transported down to London. Then at 4.00 a.m. one morning, he had it deposited in Leicester Square, with ballast in the base weighing about one ton. This made it difficult to move. He then arranged for all the newspapers to be telephoned, saying that an anonymous person had left a statue of Charlie Chaplin in Leicester Square. All the national press dispatched photographers and there was an enormous picture on the front page of every national newspaper - but nobody knew who had left it there. The police duly arrived, arrested the statue and transported it to one of their car pounds. Meanwhile, the mystery raged on. The story had Tommy Steele-practical joker written all over it. Mills remembers that after three days, Tommy phoned all the papers and said, "It's a fair cop Governor, I was responsible."

Once again, he received enormous coverage in virtually every national newspaper. Tommy had three miniatures made of the statue. He gave one to Richard Mills, he retained one for himself and the other he gave to Ian Bevan. The irony of the story is that Tommy then had the statue transported to his front courtyard. Some years later, whilst he was away on holiday, a gang of thieves with a large lorry arrived at his house and stole the statue. It has never been seen from that day to this.[424]

An Evening with Tommy Steele in Blackpool was the show that prepared him for the Prince of Wales

Theatre. It was described by Michael Parkinson as 'The show I loved.' Richard Mills refers to the Parkinson programme. He says that Tommy agreed to do the television special lasting an hour (incorporating a great deal of his show). It was broadcast on 22nd September. Watching the hour-long Parkinson spectacular was 28-year-old Michael Edgley MBE.[425]/[168] Edgley is an impresario. He saw the broadcast and said "We must bring him to Australia." With typical Australian get up and go, that is precisely what he did. Edgley described Tommy as "One of the greatest entertainers in the world today."[426]

Tommy told Sir Michael that he had deliberately stayed off television for several years until the right moment arrived. The Monday morning following the broadcast there were queues at the box office extending half-way around the block. Mills says that Tommy told him that on the day of the first night at Blackpool he was, as would be expected, extremely nervous and to take his mind off the impending show, he spent the afternoon watching the science fiction horror film *Alien*.[427]

On 15th August there was a Grand Midnight Matinee in aid of the Entertainment Artistes Benevolent Fund[169] in which Tommy participated. So, it came about that on Thursday 11th October Tommy Steele opened at the Prince of Wales theatre on Coventry Street in a *An Evening with Tommy Steele*. It opened for twelve weeks: but ended on 29th November 1980: and only closed then

---

[168] The youngest Australian ever to earn the award
[169] Now the Royal Variety Charity

since Tommy chose not to continue through the Christmas period.[428]

As one customer wrote of the show, 'The auditorium lights dimmed and the curtains rose. Suddenly hundreds of white lights dazzled around a simple stage. Tommy Steele sat at the piano and launched into Neil Sedaka's *That's When the Music Takes Me*. Within a minute I was completely gob-smacked, it was incredible, this man sold himself in less than sixty seconds. The audience went crazy and Tommy Steele's teeth got even whiter. In all the shows I have been to, this was the one I shall remember for sheer professionalism and capturing an audience.' Interestingly Mitchell, in writing about his first appearance at Sunderland in 1956, noted that even those who had entered the theatre somewhat ambivalent about Steele's abilities had been won over half way through his performance.[429]

The Daily Express wrote "Stainless Steele as bright as ever." Michael Parkinson rated it the equal of 'anything of its kind on either side of the Atlantic.' The Sunday Mirror wrote of 'Enough energy to keep four nuclear powers going.' The show itself is in the Guinness Book of Theatre Facts and Feats as the longest ever running one-man show in West End Theatre History – and when you see who else has done them, it speaks for itself. It ran for fourteen months: and four hundred and fifty-five performances.[430]

Again, there was no interval. The show constituted twenty-five songs, nine dance routines and eight costume changes. This man put on a show at 6.00 p.m. on Friday and Saturday: he went nonstop: he ended bathed in sweat.[431] He then enjoyed a half an hour break and proceeded to do it all over again. He told BBC's *Nationwide* that he had trained with the Royal Artillery on their assault course at Woolwich to get ready for the physical demands ahead. He described how he felt after their vigorous daily training regime, "It hurts: but it hurts good." Giles Brandreth wrote 'Tommy Steele is a wonderfully gifted performer: we were impressed by his skill:'[432] so they might have been.

On 20th October Tommy appeared on Noel Edmund's *Multi-Coloured Swap Shop*. The BBC trailed the spot 'Tommy Steele is a Londoner and an international star. He is at the top of the tree. He has not forgotten how he started - maybe he will give you a few tips too.'[433] It was broadcast at 9.30 a.m. in order that his daughter was able to watch it.

Christmas Day 1979[170] found Tommy talking to Sheridan Morley on *Kaleidoscope* on BBC Radio 4 in a programme styled *A Handful of Songs* about the early days of rock 'n' roll, the state of the British musical, his attitude to Hollywood; and recalling famous people he had met.

Tommy was honoured by the Variety Club of Great Britain as their chosen 1979 *Show Business Personality of the Year* at its 28th annual Awards luncheon held at the Savoy Hotel on 2nd February 1980. As noted above, he finished his long run at the Prince of Wales on

---

[170] Repeated on 21st March 1980

29th November: and it must have been time for a well-earned break.

Tommy then commenced a six-week national tour of *An Evening with Tommy Steele* staged in Britain's concert halls: commencing at Manchester's Apollo Theatre on 14th April and finishing at the Colston Hall Bristol on 24th May. In two venues - Bournemouth's Winter Gardens and Croydon's Fairfield Hall - he appeared for two nights.

Three days after the conclusion, May 27th, the Variety Club of Great Britain staged *This is Your Lunch* for Gene Kelly: among the speakers was Tommy Steele. Kelly remarked "When I put on tails, I look like a truck driver on a night out."[434]

4th July 1981 saw Tommy's rich vein of creativity continue when he achieved a real personal ambition and succeeded in having one of his paintings – *The Entertainer* – accepted for the Royal Academy's 213th Summer Exhibition. He said: "It's absolutely smashing, I am really chuffed." Prints were made of this masterpiece and he gave a signed copy to a girl named Birgita while appearing in an *Evening with Tommy Steele* in Göteborg on 8th September 1982. He had commenced painting in 1969 when he gave his wife a box of paints and she failed to use them. So, he had a go himself.[435] A further celebration was a luncheon hosted by Harold Fielding at the Lygon Arms Hotel in Broadway to celebrate Tommy's twenty-five years in showbusiness; neither Kennedy or Parnes attended. Ironic it is.

1981 continued with a further run of *Hans Andersen* this time the *5-City Tour* which kicked off at the Liverpool Empire for three weeks on 9th October and was followed by Oxford, Coventry Theatre, Southampton winding up at the Grand Theatre Leeds on the 12th December. This tour was again directed by the star. Joe Riley wrote that it was rare for a show of such quality to leave London. The Empire staff wore red carnations. The scenery was magical in what was described as a superb family show and then there was the sort of grin that makes you think that Tommy has a coat hanger stuffed in his mouth.[436]

At Leeds, the reviewer said that the Copenhagen transformation scene must be one of the best of its kind ever presented at the Grand. He went on, 'Steele is fascinating to observe with echoes of Chaplin and Astaire in his every movement. He is undoubtedly one of the great stage personalities of our time.'[437] This was to prove to be the end of a wonderful seven-year association with the musical *Hans Andersen*.

It was whilst appearing at the Liverpool Empire that Tommy made his offer to Liverpool City Council to create a sculpture as a tribute to the Beatles. His fee for the commission would be three pence. We shall come back to this.

Friday 20th November saw the 25th anniversary of Tom's career in showbusiness. The BBC broadcast a tribute programme narrated by Sir John Mills and with a script by Benny Green appropriately entitled *A Handful of Songs*.

You will remember that Tommy was watched by an Australian on the Parkinson Show in 1979. As a result, he arrived in Sydney on 1st February 1982 to appear in *The Tommy Steele Show*. He opened at Her Majesty's Theatre, Melbourne on the 26th February. On 22nd February he appeared on the *Don Lane Show.*[171] In April he moved on to the Capitol Theatre in Sydney.

He was back in the UK for 18th July when he appeared in a variety show *National Salute to the Falklands Task Force* at the London Coliseum; where he was presented to HRH Prince Charles.[438] August and September saw Tommy present an *Evening with Tommy Steele* in Stockholm and Gothenburg.

Sometime earlier, he had decided to create a statue of Eleanor Rigby as a tribute both to the Beatles and the people of Liverpool. It was meant as a 'Thank You' to the people of the city for all the happy times he had spent there: man and boy: seaman and entertainer. He produced a bronze sculpture depicting Eleanor Rigby sitting on a stone bench with a shopping bag looking down at a sparrow. He asked for a fee of 'half a sixpence' – one that he has yet to collect. Frame describes it as Steele's 'most admired and lasting contribution to rock culture:' and goes on to describe it as the most imaginative and spiritual statue in the city:'[439] what a gracious compliment.

The work cost £4,000: and was funded by the *Liverpool Echo*. The statue took nine months to make and it was unveiled by Tommy Steele on 3rd December. He

---

[171] At that time an Australian Talk Show

explained that he had placed a number of objects inside the figure, "So she would be full of *magical properties.*" Those objects were an adventure book (for excitement), a page from the Bible (for spiritual guidance), a clover leaf (for good luck), a pair of football boots (for action) and a sonnet (for love). The unveiling was a big deal for the city: a special card was issued describing its background and a souvenir envelope produced. All mail posted in Liverpool on that day being franked 'Unveiling of Eleanor Rigby statue.' It must have been a big day for Tommy Steele – broad smile and all. It got even bigger because in the evening Tommy switched on the Christmas lights on Liverpool's city centre tree and shared the joy of Christmas with eight-year-old Claire Ryan from Speke:[440] and the Spanish edition of the *Half a Sixpence* film LP was issued. You might say accurately that Tommy Steele not only lit up the sky; but also lit up the city.

March 1983 saw the publication by William Collins of *The Final Run*: a perfectly acceptable blend of espionage thriller and war novel – providing the answer to the victory of Dunkirk.[441] He wrote the tale based on a conversation that he had with a stranger on a train to Birmingham in 1982.

A Californian newspaper announced a Variety Club of Great Britain tribute – *This is Your Lunch* - to 'the all-round entertainer Tommy Steele.' Held on Thursday 15th September, it *reported that speakers included Roy Castle: and Gene Kelly*: the latter sent taped congratulations. The lunch was staged at the Savoy Hotel and the BBC broadcast highlights. The newspaper continued, 'Steele, is pulling in capacity audiences at the

London Palladium with a lavish musical, *Singin' in the Rain*.[442]

CHAPTER SEVEN

KEEP ON SINGIN'

Which leads us neatly to Tommy's next great success: *Singin' in the Rain*. Producer Harold Fielding had been negotiating with MGM in Hollywood over the rights to make a musical based on the famous film (some people say 'everyone's favourite film').[443] It has been suggested that *Singin' in the Rain* might have been the last musical of the '50s to convey irrepressible optimism through what Alan Greenspan[172] would call 'irrational exuberance.'[444]/[173] MGM did not wish to see the film turned into a stage show least of all outside the USA. But Fielding had a trump card: and the ace was Tommy Steele who would play the lead. The show was destined to open on 30th June and the entire cast had to commit themselves to a two-year minimum run. This original production was directed by Tommy Steele. It ran until September 1985 becoming, at the time, the longest running show in the history of the London Palladium.

There was a review on BBC the next day. The show was destined to be a blockbuster: although inevitably some purists criticized it. Fielding's objective always was to give the punters what *they* wanted: not to satisfy the intellectuals. Once again, the conductor was to

---

[172] Fed Chairman
[173] Unfounded optimism

be the great Michael Reed. Once more the standby for the star was Roy Sone. Tommy Steele's 1983 Palladium production used expensive special effects, pre-recorded songs and pre-recorded taps to take the pressure off its performers.[445]

The film's original vocal score was embellished with additional tunes. It was reported that because of the scale of the props Fielding would have preferred the wider stage at the Drury Lane Theatre.[446] Be that as it may, the production broke all records at the Palladium. The original plan was to take the show to New York but it was reported that Tommy had turned the part into a sort of cockney homage to Douglas Fairbanks Sr (whatever that was supposed to mean): so no way would this play on Broadway.[447] Amusingly when it opened on Broadway without Steele at the helm it failed even to cover its costs. Davies commented that the stage version became a landmark production, giving Tommy Steele one of the biggest hits in his hit-filled career.[448]

One reviewer said 'Tommy Steele's attempt made an admirable case for the viability of a stage version of the film, but largely failed to adequately transcribe the ineffable charisma behind the tap-dancing and torrential downpours that make the film so irresistible.'[449] The unpleasant Charles Spencer – Tommy Steele's most persistent and vicious critic – thought 'I have always found that a little of Tommy Steele's grinning bonhomie goes a very long way; the production almost entirely missed the charm and effervescence of the original 1952 MGM movie.'[450] That was Spencer being characteristically unkind: he lacked the capacity to understand that Tommy is not all grin and front.[451]

Johns thought Tommy a riot of misdirected energy at the Palladium in 1983:[452] which was somewhat cutting as *he* was the director. Illustrating the fact that the public loved it; but some people were kinder. Comments ranged from 'Tommy Steele's mere presence on the stage lights up the whole theatre'[453] to 'magnificently costumed, breathtakingly choreographed and mounted with exuberant panache.'[454] 'Tommy Steele's is a lovely performance; here is a player haloed by a curious radiance'[455] and the greatest compliment 'Tommy Steele can challenge the success of Gene Kelly.'[456]

The fact that it ran for so long and was so profitable, and came back to the Palladium in 1989 and went all the way to Japan suggests to this writer that this was the apotheosis of Tommy Steele's career. His OBE should have been upgraded to a knighthood much sooner than 2020 on those counts alone: in fact, Frame suggests, there is still time for him to be enobled as Lord Steele of Bermondsey:[457] there would be no more popular honour: nor would anybody add a more original mind to their lordships' debates. But, that aside, he never again rose to such great heights and those who saw the London production felt that the adverse comments were not well founded.

Next year was destined to be one long slog in the theatre. But our former merchant seaman sailed straight into 1984 in style by opening the 30th London Boat Show[174]

---

[174] An event, which, organized by British Marine, ran annually until

at the Earl's Court Exhibition Centre. He was one of a number of famous faces who had performed this ceremony over the years including the Rt Hon Edward Heath MP (1971), the Rt Hon Mrs Margaret Thatcher MP (1979) and Morecombe and Wise (1981).[458] While there, Tom tried out a dinghy in the pool. Christmas Eve 1984 saw a special edition of *Jim'll fix it for Christmas* on which Tommy danced with a young fan who wanted to dance and sing in the rain with the star.[459]

Singin' in the Rain finished its massive run at the Palladium on 28th September 1985. Tommy relates the story that his wife told him that she was fed up with his being "Someone else's night out;" accordingly he advised Harold Fielding that he wanted to end the run.

On Wednesday 6th November there was a *Royal Gala Concert* in aid of St Paul's Cathedral Choir School Foundation Appeal. It was staged at the Barbican in the presence of HRH The Duchess of Kent. The programme included the world première of Tommy's symphonic poem *A Portrait of Pablo*. Tommy conducted the London Symphony Orchestra and the choristers of the cathedral.[460]

Twenty-three days later, Tommy was interviewed by Bob Holness in a 1.00 p.m. lunchtime interview in one of the series of *Celebrity Interviews*. It was staged in Cinema 1 at the Barbican and broadcast on LBC.[461]

1986 saw the *Tommy Steele Show* in which Tommy celebrated thirty years in show business. He appeared at the Bradford Alhambra[462] which was the scene for the world première for Tom's new one-man show: a revised and re-jigged version of *An Evening with Tommy Steele*. It began an intermittent run over two years: inter alia he took his one-man show to the Blackpool Opera House on 13th July twice nightly for eight Sundays. Three years later his name appeared on a commemorative Roll of Honour at the Opera House. It was unveiled by Lord Bernard Delfont and named the many stars to have appeared there in the first one hundred years of its existence.

He was also in Denmark where he conducted the Aarhus Symphony Orchestra in another airing of *Portrait of Pablo*:[463] as he did two years later when he conducted the Odense Symphony Orchestra (and Choir) in Odense Koncerthus.[464]

One can only imagine the physical strain on the star of a lengthy run of a show like *Singin' in the Rain*. However, not yet worn out, Tommy took the show on another national tour visiting Bristol (in November 1986) and the Birmingham Hippodrome (22nd December for two months).[465] The opening in Bristol was described as triumphal: and Tommy stayed at what is now the Bristol Marriott.[466] It took three weeks to mount the scenery at Bristol and seventeen trucks were needed to transport the sets. As a result of improvements made since the staging of the show at the Palladium one hundred and fifty gallons now descended on the star and it required five driers to wring him out.[467]

The major event in 1987 was a Spring visit to Japan amidst the beauty of the cherry-blossom season:[468]

a visit that made theatrical history.⁴⁶⁹ Harold Fielding took his London production of *Singin' in the Rain* to the Shinjuku Koma Theatre[175] from the 6th April to 2nd May for thirty-five performances. This was a major logistical exercise and it took a year of intensive planning. The Flying Tiger Airline provided an open-jaw jumbo jet in which to load and fly eighty-seven tons of scenery, costumes and so forth. Incidentally, **Flying Tiger Line**[176] was the first scheduled cargo carrier in the United States: surpassing PanAm in 1980 as the world's largest air cargo carrier. It was sold to Federal Express in December 1988.⁴⁷⁰

Japan Airlines carried the contingent of seventy-six personnel. The cast stayed at the Shinjuku Prince Hotel. The Company Manager was Tony Pinhorn and the Company Code for Mr and Mrs Steele was C1.

In advance publicity, Tokyo writer Bill Hersey described Tommy as 'the multi-talented musical star' (a long way from rock 'n' roll). Hersey had enjoyed the show on Broadway and he said that he 'understood that the London production was even better;' ending 'don't miss it.'⁴⁷¹

Zac Holton was in the production. He tells a funny story. There was a brawl scene in the show, during which he had to hit Tommy over the head with a breakaway chair. It was especially designed for the purpose. During one show, while waiting for his moment, Holton realized a horrible truth. He became aware that that the chair on which he was sitting was a real one: and he was about to

---

[175] In Tokyo's red-light district: subsequently closed in 2008
[176] Also known as Flying Tigers

clobber Tommy Steele over the head with it in front of an audience.

The moment of the fight sequence arrived and Holton brushed the chair lightly down Steele's back. "What are you doing?" he whispered at me. I shook my head. "Hit me with the chair," he hissed. I shook my head again. "Hit me with the chair," he said again with some more colourful words thrown in. So, Holton did just that. He hit him with the chair and knocked him out. Holton was called to Tommy's room during the interval. "It was the longest journey from my dressing room to Tommy's," remembers Holton. He came out, puffing on a big cigar, and said: "If we are ever on stage again, no matter how much I insist, don't hit me with a chair."[472]

The highlight of 1987 - and it was a highlight indeed - was Tommy's appearance at the Royal Festival Hall in the season of *South Bank Pops '87*. Tommy himself described it as "The most exciting night of my life." Saturday 12th September saw Tom with the BBC Concert Orchestra with his old friend Michael Reed as Guest Conductor and Carlos Bonell[177] on Spanish Guitar. It was a great occasion: and an enormous personal success. The performance was broadcast later on BBC Radio 2. In the course of the programme he introduced his *Rock Suite – an Elderly Person's Guide to Rock*. He related that he learned to conduct at the Wigmore Hall: adding, "I have a pretty good sense of timing:" which is just as well. He noted that he lost the orchestra once but that he remembered that he had been told 'when in trouble

---

[177] Born in London of Spanish parents

stay with the brass.'[473] In October his show *An Evening with Tommy Steele* was on the road again appearing at the New Theatre Hull in October and the week commencing 2nd November at the Theatre Royal Norwich (which is believed to have been his only ever appearance in Norfolk).

May saw Tommy Steele - 'Britain's own International Superstar' - appearing at the New King's Cabaret Theatre which was in Hamstead, Birmingham.[474] It was badged as 'the Midland's premier Cabaret Theatre.' Premier or not it was demolished later and an Esso garage built on the site. He appeared in 'The show of the year' *The Tommy Steele Spectacular* from 3rd to 8th. He also appeared at Blazers nightclub in Windsor and at Savvas[178] in Usk: both owned by George Savva they were recognized as major cabaret venues.

Sam Russell reports that Margaret Thatcher held a reception for celebrities in 1988. Husband Denis questioned the inclusion of Sebastian Coe, Shirley Bassey and magician Paul Daniels on the list of people to be invited. Ticks and question marks were put against some names. The names of other artists - actors and athletes such as Tommy Steele, Daley Thompson, John Barnes and Julian Fellowes - received no markings at all.[475] So one supposes that he was acceptable, in a manner of speaking.

In early summer 1988 Harold Fielding launched his new musical *Ziegfeld*.[179] Budgeted at $5.9 million, the

---

[178] Previously, the Stardust Club
[179] Based upon the life of Florenz Ziegfeld, an American Broadway

production received poor notices from British critics.[476] The London reviews were horrendous. Michael Billington of The Guardian summed up the show as 'expensive nothingness.' Michael Coveney of The Financial Times called it 'a sad litany of disconnected items.' Jack Tinker of The Daily Mail found fault with almost everything and everyone: from a plot resembling 'a great hole' to Mr. Cariou, whom he accused of 'such bland self-effacement that it amounts to anonymity.' 'Brains should be checked in with the coats,' he concluded. Well that took care of that.

Fielding carried out changes. One leading reviewer summed up its reworking, its restaging and the replacement in the title role of Len Cariou by the Israeli actor Topol as like 'rearranging the furniture on the Titanic.'[477]

By 16th May the cast also had a second director, replacing Joe Layton, the American who had left Britain just after the opening. The newcomer was an old trouper: none other than Tommy Steele, a veteran of many Fielding shows. He had seen *Ziegfeld* and concluded, he said, that "It's 80% marvellous but 20% awfully wrong."[180] He telephoned the producer's office offering his help, then turned up with five pages of suggestions.[478] Scenes were cut, songs added and tap dance routines inserted. The ideas took him until 4.00 a.m.[479] But Tom's efforts were not enough to save the day and the show closed with

---

impresario; famous for his series of theatrical revues
[180] Sometimes quoted as 90% and 10%.

enormous losses: which partly helped to secure the bankruptcy of poor Fielding in 1990.

In 1989 *Singin in the Rain* re-appeared at the Manchester Palace for a very long run: it was a sell-out and smashed box office records. Then it was revived at the London Palladium for thirteen weeks from the 29th June: but this was extended by popular demand through 18th November: in all 164 performances. It had to finish on that date because of other Palladium commitments: and that was the end of *Singin' in the Rain.*

There is an interesting side note to all this. As noted, the production had been on tour and was due to play this season at the Palladium starring Tim Flavin,[181] but Flavin fractured his foot during rehearsals. Tommy Steele agreed to step in at the last moment.[480]

---

[181] The first American actor to be presented with the Laurence Olivier Award

CHAPTER EIGHT

JUST ONE OF LIFE'S
<u>BAD MOMENTS</u>

It was announced that Tom, who had been preparing for this project for several years and who had originated the idea, was to star in and direct *Some Like it Hot*. It was Harold Fielding who had persuaded those controlling the copyright of Wilder's film and Merrick's musical *Sugar* (which in spite of a number of pre-production problems had managed to run for 505 performances in New York) to allow a stage presentation under the title *Some Like it Hot*: a right that had always been refused before. Mark Furness took over the project in 1990 when a new book was written together with new songs.[481] This version was heavily revised, with the emphasis switched from the character of Sugar to the show's star and director, Tommy Steele. Tommy flew to New York in 1990 and worked closely with Styne on both the score and the book. Rehearsals began in 1991.[482]

It opened for a provincial tour on 16th June 1991: for three weeks at the Churchill Theatre Bromley, it went on to the Bristol Hippodrome and the Manchester Opera House (14th August - 21st September), the Liverpool Empire (25th September – 10th October); the Sunderland Empire (20th January 1992 – 1st February): Theatre Royal Plymouth (5th - 22nd February). It was a great success wherever it went in the provinces. Here is a flavour of the review of the first night in Manchester: 'It positively sizzles. This is the kind of show they do not make any more; featuring spot on choreography that is rare on this side of the Atlantic. It has success written all over it. Steele plays the Tony Curtis role and is sensational. The songs are not the strongest part but the *Flash, Bang, Wallop!* man has done it again.'[483]

'He gives them what they want: a spectacle of the highest quality.'[484] The late - and much lamented - Megan Tresidder[182] saw the production in Plymouth and wrote about it at length for the *Sunday Times*. The best part she said was Tommy Steele 'tap dancing and singing with his blue-eyed boyish radiance. He provided the corniest night but of the highest calibre.'[485]

The production then translated to the Prince Edward Theatre, London with previews on the 2nd March opening on the 19th: it had closed by mid-June. The project ended in disaster: and in substantial losses for those who invested in the show. Apparently, it lost over £2 million.[486] The final straw was a bad injury suffered by the 55-year-old star when he badly bruised his back in a motor cycle accident on stage. Tommy was forced to withdraw from the cast following the accident; as a result, the show soon closed.

It was damned by most of the London critics. One wrote 'Well, some may like it hot; but this show seems better suited to those who prefer it lukewarm. Billy Wilder's original movie had a bright, quick wit that lifted its transvestite drolleries way above pantomime level.

---

[182] She died in 2001 aged 42

That spark is all but snuffed out by its transformation into a conventional musical, complete with lavish sets and stage effects, brash yet anodyne melodies, jaunty production numbers and, not least, Tommy Steele's celebrated teeth. Mr Steele's Joe is essentially the same boy-next-door all his Joes and Johns have been since *Half a Sixpence* in 1963.'[487] As for Tommy himself – he made a few excuses for the early demise but said: "It's not worth printing them - a flop is a flop."[488]

Another reviewer wrote 'It seems churlish to carp at a £2 million show that has a massive £1.5 million advance. People have clearly come to see a Tommy Steele show rather than a misguided musical version of the classic Billy Wilder comedy. This production, directed by and starring Steele, is a gaudy and mediocre travesty of an immortal movie comedy. It is not even redeemed by good songs, since Jule Styne and Bob Merrill obviously had a lacklustre day when they worked on this. The delicious wit and exuberant satire of the original are largely lost in this musical massacre. Tommy Steele and Billy Boyle never even approach the foothills of Tony Curtis and Jack Lemmon's magnificent twin peaks.'[489] A third – unknown - remarked unkindly 'the hero is Mr Steele's dentist.'

So: why the failure? There might have been a degree of overconfidence at the start in both the project and in Tommy's ability as a director. The tunes were not catchy: they were actually quite poor. Tommy always tended to come across as Tommy Steele and critics were increasingly unengaged by the smile of the London cockney. Perhaps it was the wrong show at the wrong time. Maybe society and tastes had changed and those behind the project failed to realize it. Whatever the answer, the brightness of Tommy Steele's allure never shone as sharply again.

It is an ill wind that blows no one any good. On 29th October 1993 Tommy unveiled his concrete sculpture *Union* attached to the back of the East Stand at Twickenham. He had contacted the RFU and told them of his love of rugby. Apparently, the authority had some unease about the idea[490] but the sculpture ended up being welcomed warmly. It now features proudly on an *Arts Tour* of the stadium.[491] Tommy knew Henry Moore and met him at the dentist, as one does. Moore said "How do" and asked him if he had seen the programme about Modigliani[183] on BBC2 the night before, which, of course, Tommy had. Moore told him that sculpture has to be touched: 'You have to see it against a cobalt blue sky and feel where the sculptor has been to understand.' Tommy went into the Tate and felt Moore's *Reclining Nude.* An attendant objected. "Listen, mate," Tommy told him, "The fella who did this told me to touch it, so I'm touching it."[492]

1993 saw an award – if not from the UK – from Denmark when Tommy was presented with the *Hans Andersen Award* at the Danish Embassy. He also appeared on one of Eddie Skoller's shows for Danish and Swedish television on 21st April 1994.[184] Skoller recalled his first meeting with Tommy Steele[493] at London's Waldorf Hotel.[185] He remembered Tommy had been

---

[183] Italian Jewish painter and sculptor whose work is mainly in France
[184] Skoller is an American-Danish entertainer who debuted at Visevershuset in Copenhagen's Tivoli Gardens
[185] Now the Waldorf Hilton

dressed immaculately and his being more cultured and knowledgeable (particularly about history) than he had expected. Skoller thought him a very nice person. He notes that Tommy's management were very protective of their star in particular making demands regarding his dressing room. In spite of this rigour, the two of them became good friends. He described Tommy as 'old school and super professional with great respect for his job' – which is probably what got up the noses of the stage hands at the London Palladium. Tommy himself commented that "With all the greats with whom I have worked, they all had the same thing in common – the need to get it right."[494] Interestingly, Hardy quotes Tommy's publicist who also describes him as 'old school:' saying 'professionalism, self-discipline and good manners are his touchstones.'[495] Remember that Charles Spencer.

In tandem, the 1983 London Palladium production of *Singin' in The Rain* was remounted for an extensive tour of the United Kingdom, which ran until December 1995. The new production starred Paul Nicholas but was again directed by Tommy Steele.

Tom, with his back now fully recovered, was working on his next blockbuster - 'A Dazzling New Song and Dance Spectacular[496] – *What a Show!* Monday 21st March 1994 Tommy was billed to be at the Birmingham Hippodrome for two weeks in *The Very Best of Tommy Steele* – but in the event this became *What a Show!*

Tommy promoted *What a Show!* on 9th February on *Des O'Connor Tonight*. It opened in Dartford in March and toured nineteen cities before opening in London on 9th

October 1995 running through the 6th January. There were to be no world records this time. His third date was in Southampton where *Southampton News* bellowed 'He's back with a bang.'

The sad fact is that, as with *Some Like it Hot*, the provinces were kinder than the capital. Typical of the London notices was 'The title of Tommy Steele's whistle-stop tour of his four decades as an all-round entertainer verges on hubris.[186] The large fan club contingent in the first night audience was predictably rapturous; elsewhere, though, could be spotted a frozen-jawed rictus of disbelief. Steele's ego pervades every aspect of the show. His name looms above the title; no director is credited (we infer that it is Tommy's baby); most ridiculously, the cast list in the programme is precisely one name long. The applause is to be Tommy's alone.'

But Charles Nevin in a generous and understanding review of *What a Show!* described it as 'a megamix of the Steele career, his greatest hits, chat, song and dance, tooth and hoof; and Tommy flirting and playing to the audience as shamelessly as ever; defying age and aspirates, crinkling the eyes, shaking the head, hand on the heart.' He went on the 'applause from a full house in Wimbledon rolled up at him from the blazers, bald patches and perms who were young when he was young and have aged as he has not aged.[497] Nevin captured the appeal of this ordinary cockney sprite - with

---

[186] Extreme pride or dangerous overconfidence, often in combination with arrogance.

his people - in the way that no metropolitan liberal could hope to do.

Another writer said 'The Bermondsey boy knows how to put a show together. The assemblage of numbers, winsome gags and audience-charming sessions is the kind of variety package one did not think was made any more. His ensemble, changing costumes several times from traditional chorus-line drag to cartoon cockney for *Flash, Bang, Wallop!* to Lycra-mediaeval for *The King's New Clothes,* disport themselves with vast energy and fixed grins. Tommy Steele undeniably knows his craft, but on the evidence of *What a Show!* he can either no longer pull it off or, more worryingly, has come to believe that after so long, adulation is his as of right. It is not'. You pays your money and you takes your choice.[498]

At the same time, Richardson relates, after taking his artwork to a framers Tom was told fine art dealers Frost and Reed of Bond Street had taken an interest in his work. Within weeks two hundred and fifty prints were on sale. The dealers staged a successful exhibition of Tommy's paintings, drawings and sculpture to honour his forty years in entertainment: with a Preview on Wednesday the 25th October.[499]

The real drama in 1995 was precipitated by a malicious story printed in the News of the World in July suggesting a close friendship between Sue Phipps, a saxophonist in *What a Show!* and Tommy Steele. The paper did a comprehensive job of lampooning the star describing his happy marriage as a lot of *Little White Bull.* It was a sign that the respect for the star had waned in some quarters. Very sensibly he declined to comment on the matter at the time; he has done so ever since. On a happier note, 1995 saw a further honour when Tommy was presented with the *Bernard Delfont Award for Outstanding Contribution to Showbusiness*.

1995 also saw the broadcast of a four-part series on BBC Radio 2 relating the story of the legendary impresario Harold Fielding: it began on 14th November. There was no one better qualified to write and present the tribute.

The end of 1996 saw a low-keyed celebration of Tommy's 40th year in showbusiness. A number of long-time fans gathered at the Richmond Gate Hotel[187] where they were joined by Tom and his wife. He gave all those attending a signed print of *Take a Bow*. In addition to being a very convivial occasion it was one of the first when he was photographed wearing spectacles. The event was organized by Alan and Janet Smith who, at that time, ran his Fan Club.

1998 saw another regurgitation of An Evening with Tommy Steele: not this time What a Show! but Tommy Steele in Concert. It was staged at the Princess Theatre Torquay (23rd April), Birmingham Hippodrome, Ipswich Regent (3rd May) and the Playhouse Edinburgh (11/12th May): and he took it to Denmark.[500] However, far more importantly London South Bank University awarded him an honorary Doctor of Literature and he became Dr Tommy Steele OBE ~~~ a far cry from poverty in Frean Street.

---

[187] Now the Richmond Harbour

May 1999 saw Tommy in Cornwall for the first time for many years: possibly only the second time since he was evacuated there during the war. Incidentally, while there he attended Basset Road Secondary School and became its most famous 'old boy.'[501] He starred at the *Daphne du Maurier Festival of Arts and Literature* centred in Fowey (his performance was billed as 'his only UK performance this year');[502] appearing at the grandiosely named Cornwall Coliseum[188] where he staged his one-man show for one night. One elderly woman who had known him during the war met him after the show. We believe that it was the last time that he staged this show on English soil: it was well received in front of a good audience of people who had travelled from all over the county (and indeed further).

---

[188] It was located on Carlyon Bay near St Austell - and demolished in 2015

CHAPTER NINE

A DICKENS OF A WONDERFUL CHRISTMAS!

There were stories in the press about the next event as early as 1988.[503] In September 1999, Tommy appeared at the Old Fire Station in Oxford – it is a charity-run culture hub showcasing contemporary U.K. drama and music. *Chaplin The Musical* was tried out there.[504] Richardson recalls both a small intimate theatre and being two metres from the players: Ian Lavender[189] was in the audience. For whatever reason the project went no further.[505]

We believe that Tommy saw in the Millennium on Cunard's Queen Elizabeth 2 *Millennium Cruise*: and appeared on stage: a programme for this alleged performance appeared for sale on eBay some years ago at an inflated price. He was later in Oslo at the Koncerthus on Sunday 29th October 2000 with *Tommy Steele and Orchestra in Concert.* Tommy also appeared on Sweden's Bingolotto show in 2000 and sang *Singin' the Blues* and *A Handful of Songs*.[506]

One thing of which we are certain is that for centuries the tower of Southwark Cathedral provided the best views across the Thames between the Cities of London and Westminster. It is from here that the Bohemian artist Wenceslas Hollar[190] drew the definitive panorama of

---

[189] Best remembered as the *Stupid Boy* in *Dad's Army*

historic London: his *Long View of London*. In 2001 the cathedral opened a new exhibition housed in the Old Refectory. Using state-of-the-art technology, it allows visitors to take a 'Long View of London' and especially Southwark. Touch-screen computers enable visitors to discover artefacts uncovered during recent excavations at the Cathedral. There is a specially commissioned audio tour. This was recorded, using the vocal talents of Peter Barker, Prunella Scales, Tommy Steele, Timothy West and Zoë Wanamaker.[507] It is terrific.

Yet again Tommy appeared at Copenhagen's Tivoli Gardens in July 2001 with *Tommy Steele in Concert:* this may have been his last ever presentation of his one-man show. One unidentified person present wrote in broken English: 'On a chair right on the stage, he sits under a sharp spotlight and brings *The Ugly Duckling* alive. He is the duckling who makes sure not to be like the others. He tells the Hans Andersen story to the audience in the Glass Hall in Tivoli. His face is drawn in folds worthy of a distrustful duckling, and the mimicry is clear and precise. Admittedly, 64-year-old Tommy Steele is best known as the first European rock 'n' roll singer who made a lot of teenage girls scream but it only took him three years to become tired of being a rock idol. I loved the scenes, the limelight, the orchestras and the applause of the audience. With the glass velvet red and flashing prisms as the right variety Tommy Steele sings, dances and acts in the evening with an orchestra that is all about swinging, chatting and telling good, old adventures. Broadly smiling

---

[190] Czech born, he is particularly noted for his engravings and etchings

Tommy Steele presents a tour of the highlights of his forty-five years in showbiz. He has all the jokes, stories and songs from musicals like *Half a Sixpence* and *Hans Andersen*. But he manages to deliver them with that little extra charm in the still-guilty eyes; reminiscent of Gene Kelly.'

In 2003, Arthur Johnson, former Marketing Editor of the Liverpool Echo, helped arrange a 21st birthday party for the Eleanor Rigby sculpture. Tommy was appearing at the Empire at the time and met some of his old shipmates at the statue's birthday party. Now the bad news. The statue plaque has been stolen twice: along with some other parts:[508] people obviously enjoy stealing artefacts connected with Tommy Steele.

Later in the year, to the general surprise of his admirers, Tommy reappeared on stage for the first time since the ill-fated *Some Like it Hot* in 1992 (other than in his one-man show). Having become friends with Bill Kenwright and given up playing squash, Tommy had started playing tennis with Kenwright's partner, actress Jenny Seagrove. The story goes - according to Mandrake in the Sunday Telegraph - that she was instrumental in suggesting that he played the lead in a new musical production of *Scrooge*:[509] Lesley Bricusse's musical adaptation of Charles Dickens' classic *A Christmas Carol*. So, it came about that he opened on Thursday 16th October 2003 at the Birmingham Hippodrome Theatre. Tommy has often, rightly or wrongly, described the part of Scrooge as the song and dance man's King Lear.

The musical had first appeared in Birmingham in 1992. It was created as a vehicle for the late Anthony Newley. The Sunderland Journal, as usual, gave him a warm welcome 'a fast moving, all singing, all dancing production had the audience gasping and cheering.'[510] Tommy was asked to describe the appeal of the show. He responded, "Firstly, the sound of the orchestra, it is wonderful. Then the set appears and that is London Cheapside and it is breath-taking and everything happens within the confines of that set which is why so much money has been lavished on it. Then the company start to appear on the set and they just keep on coming, it's a huge cast, adults and children. Then they start to sing and the audience hear this wonderful choral sound. Then you get the story, one of the best things Dickens ever wrote. Then the ghosts appear. Every time a ghost appears the show goes up another level and another twenty decibels. It's magical, all those ingredients plus a great score. It's a lovely show, that's why I keep doing it and that's why I'll keep on doing it – as long as they keep asking me."[511]

A bizarre story hit the headlines on 21st April 2004 when American filmmaker Quentin Tarantino[191] suddenly announced that he was a "Huge fan of Tommy Steele" and declared that he had ambitions to work with him. Asked which British actor he would most like to use in one of his films, Tarantino - the cult director of *Pulp Fiction* and *Reservoir Dogs* - had chosen Tommy without hesitation. "I've always liked Tommy Steele," the director said. "When I think of him, I think of that Disney movie, *The Happiest Millionaire*."[512] Tommy responded "I wish

---

[191] Known for violent films

he would. I'd love to kill someone on the screen."[513] An unlikely scenario for this cheeky, chirpy song and dance man. This was like a Kennedy story: needless to say, nothing more was ever heard of the matter.

Still in 2004 a Blue Plaque was unveiled at Nickleby House on the Dickens Estate in Bermondsey to mark the place where Tommy Steele lived between 1937 and 1944 (except for his enforced absence in Cornwall as an evacuee). Having been bombed out of two houses in Mason Street his family had moved into the bottom floor in a block of flats: and there was a strong feeling of community in the area.[514] Tommy said "It is a wonderful honour; Bermondsey gave me something that I shall always treasure." Mitchell forcibly made the point that it always seemed to matter a great deal to Steele that he should retain the respect of his community.[515] Another thing that materialized in 2004 was Tommy's appearance on *Children in Need* singing *Thank you Very Much* – the big number from *Scrooge the Musical*.

9th June 2005 Tommy unveiled a plaque erected in his honour in the Cinderella Bar at the London Palladium marking the fact that, taking all his diverse appearances into account, he had headlined more shows in the history of the theatre than any other artiste.[516]

Tommy returned to London's West End in 2006 in *Scrooge* at the Palladium. On 17th October Edward Seckerson[192] talked to him about his fifty-year career: as The Daily Telegraph commented; 'Fings aint wot they

---

[192] Writer and musical theatre obsessive

used to be' when Tommy Steele is interviewed on BBC Radio 3.[193]/517

So, the scene was set for the worst theatre review that Tommy ever received. It was written by the Daily Telegraph's theatre critic Charles Spencer. It was not sober: and it was extreme. It was not a review but an unprecedented personal attack on the star. It reflected as badly on the writer as it should not have done on a show which had given pleasure to many paying customers around the country.

Shenton wrote: 'Recently, Charles Spencer went several steps too far in reviewing not just Tommy Steele's current performance in *Scrooge* but his entire past reputation. He wrote: 'Though Steele is almost invariably described as a 'much-loved entertainer,' I have never met anyone (with the exception of this show's producer, Bill Kenwright) who admits to liking him, let alone loving him.' Spencer repeated a showbiz legend – that when Tommy appeared in *Singin' in the Rain* at the Palladium, he was so disliked by the backstage crew that they would regularly urinate into the water tanks that were to rain down on to Steele's head during his performance of the show's title number.

The writer continued 'In what amounted to a total demolition of Steele's talents, he hardly left himself any room, as he himself admitted, to review the production. The result is that both the production and the reader were failed. And so was the critical art – we have a privileged

---

[193] The old Third Programme would never have deigned to interview Tommy Steele

position of power and we must be vigilant against allowing our personal opinions not merely to cloud our critical judgement but entirely overwhelm them. A review like this does not speak for us all.'[518] On a happier note Sir Ian McKellen attended the final performance of the first run of *Scrooge* at the Palladium and visited the star backstage.[519] Presumably he, like Kenwright, liked (and enjoyed) both the musical and the star.

2006 saw the publication of *Bermondsey Boy* the first volume of Tommy's autobiography. Although further volumes have been written they have not been published. Its style and language would not appeal to everyone. The fact is that it is a delightful account of Tommy's life up to the point where he decided to abandon rock 'n' roll. It gives a very real flavour of what it was like growing up in dockland during and after The War – particularly for the benefit of others who grew up in different environments. Above all, it provides a very real picture of his mother and father and conveys in eloquent language his affection for both of them. They come across as people with whom it would have been a privilege to spend time.

26th October the BBC celebrated the fiftieth anniversary of the issue of *Rock with the Caveman* with a thirty-minute programme on Radio 2 *The Birth of British Rock and Roll.*

Tommy presumably having tired of *Scrooge*, began the first of several tours of *Dr Dolittle*. He was asked about it and said that it was the best family show in which he had appeared: that was publicity hype. This writer takes it with a pinch of salt: fairly good it was, outstanding it was not. It did not stand comparison with *Cinderella, Dick Whittington* or *Hans Andersen*. Another instance of the same hyperbole was that he told the Guardian that the show represented "All my dreams come true"[520] which if correct would say little for his dreams. Having said that, he remarked that when he watched the film, he felt it was not the right thing for him: he thought it too slow. But Kenwright had the show rewritten for him with some new songs. He talked at the time of the production going to Broadway. This, of course, never happened: and this writer believes that it would not have survived the transition.[521]

An unknown reviewer commented 'Tommy is now seventy and I do not think that there is a more consummate performer alive today. You have to go if only to see him.' The writer proceeded to wonder aloud why on earth he had not been knighted. A London reviewer said 'in a word it is another Tommy Steele Show. Mr Steele has developed into a suave, competent actor-comedian with a surprisingly charming light tenor voice.'[522] Most people reading this would understand instinctively what the writer meant by a 'Tommy Steele Show' – the expression resonates with expectations of an entertaining and cheerful evening in the theatre: time well spent. The writer commented that Tommy pulled the production together with great élan and proved that 'star quality still exists and can make a show.'

The Royal Naval Museum at Portsmouth was very excited in 2009 when Tommy visited whilst he was appearing at the Mayflower Southampton. He had not been there for thirty years and was interested to see the changes: the staff noticed his uncanny resemblance to Admiral Nelson.[523] Perhaps he should have written a musical based on Nelson's life and starred in it himself.[524]

Karen Overbury from the Journal commented on his re-appearance at Sunderland. You could have bottled the festive warmth after the final curtain.'[525] David Munro thought 'it sweeps you off your feet. The star is an amazing tour de force. He held the audience in the palm of his hand.'[526]

Tommy tells a delightful story of when he was appearing at the Sunderland Empire in 2007: which readers who know the north east will understand. He was told - quite rightly - to go to Whitley Bay to enjoy the best fish and chips in the world. He went to Newcastle Central and got a taxi to Whitley Bay. He found the café and had a wonderful fish meal. He emerged at 3.30 p.m. and made his way back to the taxi rank. It was raining like hell and there were no taxis. "Get the Metro," he was told. He got on a train which ended before Newcastle. He eventually arrived back in Sunderland at 7.30 p.m. Moral: do not try to go to Whitley Bay on a Sunday by train and taxi.

After several manifestations *Scrooge* reappeared in Dublin for the Christmas season of December 2010. It began a run at the New Wimbledon Theatre in that October. A reviewer commented 'his Ebenezer Scrooge is perfection. He is exactly the character delineated by Dickens; his dancing is now reduced to a few steps; but these he executes with grace and panache. This is a joyous festive show enhanced by a matchless performance by Tommy Steele.'[527] The reduced dancing would certainly have been exacerbated by hip problems: Fryer referred in 2018 to his having two new hips:[528] surely no surprise in the light of the punishment to which they had been subjected over the years.

Honour after honour fell upon Tommy. In April 2013, the Rotherhithe and Bermondsey Local History Society – which aims to encourage interest in the history of Rotherhithe, Bermondsey, the surrounding area, Docklands and the River Thames – appointed Tommy Steele OBE as the society's first Patron. His appointment was endorsed by a packed meeting in April. He was described as 'an amazingly multi-talented individual.'[529] Quite so.

CHAPTER TEN

75
STILL GOING STRONG

On Boxing Day 2011 Don Black celebrated Tommy's 75th birthday on BBC Radio 2.[530] Eighteen months later, on 26th July 2013, Tommy Steele, as himself a distinguished former mariner, honoured retired mariners at the Queen Victoria Seamen's Rest 170th anniversary. Before an audience of more than two hundred people he awarded six ageing seamen with medals including the United Kingdom Merchant Navy Veteran Badge and the Royal Navy Armed Forces Badge. A specially commissioned canvas by the son of one of the badge recipients, Barry Andrews, was also unveiled at the event at the East India Dock Road. The Charity said 'We were delighted that Tommy Steele was able to share this day with us. It was a wonderful day and a fitting tribute to a charity that has served a community for one hundred and seventy years.'[531]

Come the 28th August 2015 (through 5th September) Tommy kicked off at the Wimbledon New Theatre starring in the *Glenn Miller Story*: an initial run ending at the New Theatre Cardiff (9th/14th November). The story is now well told. For several years producer Bill Kenwright and Tommy Steele have enjoyed dining together every so many months. Tommy gave a lecture to some secondary school pupils about rock 'n' roll and country music: a young girl, who was probably about twelve, asked him what it was like to sing with Glenn Miller, to which he laughed and said, "I'm not that old." He told this story to Bill Kenwright who said, "That's it …. the Glenn Miller Story."[532] It was when discussing the famous Glenn Miller that Tommy revealed that he had an enduring love for his music. Tommy had seen him at the Royal Albert Hall as a small child. Kenwright learned that he travelled all over the world to hear the sound.

Tommy reckoned that Glenn Miller changed the face of music from 1939 – 1943 when he had become the most popular recording artiste in the world. Kenwright thought that putting Tommy Steele and Glenn Miller together might be a winning combination. The problem, as Tommy perceived it, was that he was too old to play Miller. The answer, Kenwright thought, was for Tommy to narrate the famous story. So, it came about that Tommy found himself backed by a first rate live sixteen-piece orchestra together with a company of singers and dancers.

The late Penny Flood interviewed Tom in 2015. She wrote 'the first thing that struck me about Tommy was his charm, he is a natural, he exudes it. The next thing that surprised me was his age; he's nearly eighty but he does not look it, he's slim and fit, and full of energy. The blond locks are grey now and he wears reading glasses, but the blue eyes still twinkle and when he smiles it's the old Tommy Steele smile.'[533]

18th July 2016 Tommy Steele was honoured as an 'Adopted Scouser.' He was presented with a *Spirit of*

Liverpool Liver Bird by the Lord Mayor of Liverpool to recognize his enduring affection for the people of that great city. This real affection had been exemplified by his creation of the Eleanor Rigby statue in the city centre. The Lord Mayor commented that Tommy had given the city an iconic sculpture and it seemed only fitting that the City should demonstrate their affection for him. Tommy noted "I have a great love for Liverpool; I used to sail from Liverpool and most of my shipmates were Scousers. My career has had some wonderful moments in Liverpool and my friends at the Press Club taught me so much about handling the press. I've always been grateful to the city and its people."[534]

Elliot Davis, the prolific music documentary maker for the BBC, wrote a celebration of Tommy's life – inevitably *A Handful of* Songs - which was presented by Bill Kenwright and broadcast on 27th December 2016

When the Glenn Miller Story moved on to the London Coliseum in 2018 for a short season it was nice to read one generous review: 'As soon as Tommy Steele walks alone on to the stage at the London Coliseum, you realise that you are in the presence of showbiz royalty. The reaction from the audience is pure joy; he clearly knows that he has the audience in the palm of his hand. He chats effortlessly about his career and informs us that he made his legitimate stage debut in 1958 starring in Rodgers and Hammerstein's Cinderella, which enjoyed a sold-out run at this very theatre, jokingly adding, 'it has only taken sixty years for the management to invite me back' (which is one of Tom's corniest and most boring jokes). It continued: 'Tommy Steele is approaching his eighty second birthday but this is an irrelevance as he is the narrator of the *Glenn Miller Story*. But ultimately it is Tommy Steele's show and why not? It is not often you get to see a showbiz legend doing what he does at his brilliant best. Long may our very own Bermondsey boy continue.'[535] It was written in a style from which Charles Spencer might have taken a lesson.

15th October there was quite a stir in Great Marlborough Street. An all-new art installation by Lee Simmons entitled the *Wall of Fame* was unveiled as part of the renovated façade of the London Palladium. It was a ceremony led by Andrew Lloyd Webber. The *Wall* is located at the Palladium's world-famous stage door. It will serve as a permanent legacy to the many stars who have headlined the venue. Tommy, as the man who had headlined more shows at the Palladium than any other, was present at the ceremony.[536] In the event, to the casual observer, the *Wall* is something of a disappointment.

Thursday 7th November 2019 at the Lansdowne Club in Berkeley Square there was a special luncheon to celebrate Tommy's life and career. At the time, eighty-two years old and still passionate about performing, the star was honoured with a lifetime achievement award by the *British Music Hall Society*.

Among those present were his close friend and chairman of Everton Bill Kenwright and Richard M. Mills. Sir Tim Rice and Dr Harry Brunjes[194] were guest speakers. Dr Brunjes is Chairman of The London Coliseum where Tommy appeared in 1958 and 2018. He

---

[194] Chairman of English National Opera

made much reference to this in his speech including the fact that he had booked Tommy for the Christmas season of 2078 so as to continue the sequence!

In responding, this multi-talented veteran of show business said that he would never lose his desire to put on a show; he added "I can make them laugh, cry and make them get scared. If there are people out there, the ambition is to be able to entertain them." The meal comprised a three-course lunch and tickets were priced at £100 for non-members.[537/538]

Only two weeks later, 1st December, Tom was star of a special event at the British Film Institute[195] where he presented *Magical Moments of the Musicals;* a whirlwind tour of the genre: of which evidentially he could claim to have both knowledge and experience. On his feet and entertaining the audience with jokes and stories he took them through his personal choice of musical film highlights.

In 1959, MacInnes referred to Tom as an intensely creative person.[539] Sixty-one years later, 2020 saw the polymath power on! While the nation was in lock-down following the Chinese plague, Tommy busied himself writing and recording a Second World War thriller which he published as *Breakheart.* He announced its forthcoming publication with a specially recorded video. The story was available exclusively online throughout May 2020. For those who enjoy war time thrillers and have an interest in WWII it was compulsive listening: a

---

[195] A film and charitable organisation promoting filmmaking and television in the United Kingdom

seven-part audio thriller, a new episode was released each day for a week on YouTube.[196]

A fitting conclusion to this account of the lifetime of a golden star was the announcement in the 2020 Queen's Birthday Honours[197] of a long overdue knighthood for a star who had given so much pleasure to so many millions of people over sixty-four years. Royal Central boasted the headline "Arise Sir Tommy:" some people had waited many years to hear the news. The star told the PA News Agency that he was 'living in a show business fairy story.' He was honoured for services to entertainment and charity (he had given much support to The Salmon Youth Centre in Bermondsey which has been supporting young people in inner city London for over a hundred years). There was a palpable and universal sense of rejoicing.

---

[196] https://www.youtube.com/watch?v=Ffe48nE-vMU

[197] Delayed because of the Covid-19 crisis

ENCORE

Victor Lasky wrote a penetrating analysis of John F. Kennedy. He entitled it *JFK: The Man and the Myth.* Much of the myth concerning Tommy Steele originated from fake news in the early days. For example, he told Nunn that he did not go to church but believed in God and prayed every day.[540] This writer suspects that a publicist was behind this assertion. By 2006 he was telling Mary Riddell that his 'faith in God was finally crushed by the painful death from cancer of his mother soon after he had bought her a retirement home with a beautiful lawn in Kent'[541] at Bickley.'[198] It would not have been helped by the death of his sister Sandra from the same disease in 2005.

In 1960, at the time that Tommy was appearing in *She Stoops to Conquer*, NME hired a famous London Palmist to read an anonymous pair of hands. Some of her comments were illuminating. She opined: 'he puts everything he has into his work; he will live to a ripe old age: he will be a terrific success all the way: he is very rich and will always have money: his hands seem to express themselves constantly: he loves his parents and his family: he is very close to his sister: he is a bouncy light hearted person: he is doing something unusual and the letter **S** keeps flashing before me: he is slim, medium

---

[198] Where his sister Sandra was married in 1967

height and shows big teeth when he smiles.' It was a pretty good analysis.[542]

So, to the man. To savour Steele's art you must really see him – not just listen to recordings – to see him is to observe a thoroughly engaging theatrical personality with an enormous inborn power of self-projection onto his audience.[543] These God given talents have allowed him by 2020 to have become 'one of the most successful and enduring entertainers of all time.'[544]

So, it is due time to try to appraise the life's work of this multi-talented entertainer. Despite the extent of his success in the late 1950s, Tommy has seldom been accorded much attention by popular music commentators or historians[545] to which Mitchell might have added 'respect.' It is astonishing, nay scandalous, that his heroic achievements in this period have almost been air brushed away. Tommy was a rock 'n' roll singer for only two and a quarter years; but it is a matter of record that with so little time devoted to that part of his career he should be credited with enough firsts and innovations to fill a lifetime devoted to the craft.[546]

It needs to be understood that there are some pseudo intellectuals who consider that anything before 1963 was not rock 'n' roll: whereas the actuality is that between 1955 and 1958 the music actually was rock 'n' roll: much of what came after was neither rock nor roll. In 2006 Tommy celebrated half a century in the business. It was almost ignored, not least by the honours committee. Smurthwaite observed that 'in spite of the fact that Steele had done absolutely everything as a performer and artiste;

been everywhere, met everyone, and made pots of money in the process; 'there was a marked lack of interest in his anniversary.'[547]

Everitt posed an interesting question. He wondered aloud 'what has he got that the others have not got?' Writing in 1958, he said that show business in general has worried itself trying to answer these questions. He considered that nobody so lacking in technical ability and experience had ever risen to the top income bracket on the British stage as fast as Tommy Steele. He reckoned that he (in the form of Tommy Steele Promotions) had taken home more than £25,000 after tax in his first year. Everitt answered his own question. He reckoned that Kennedy bulldozed theatre management into booking Steele and missed no opportunity for publicity.[548] However, bear in mind MacInnes noting that 'a real talent outlasted the ballyhoo.'[199]/[549]

Frame writes generously of post rock 'n' roll Steele. He comments that Tommy continued to astound all his old cronies with the intrepid bounds he made in showbusiness and he was greatly responsible for his own expansion once he had other areas to explore. Frame wonders first whether anyone led a fuller life in the last fifty years of the century; and, secondly, was there no activity in which this unassuming polymath[200] could not excel.[550] Name any stage or screen star of the past five decades and, chances are, Steele has worked with them. An unknown writer described him as a man who knew his

---

[199] Of rock 'n' roll
[200] One who excels across a wide and diverse range of areas

trade, his audience and had, in a way, turned down an immensely successful career in the USA to return to his roots:[551] an interesting point in the age of the *Brain Drain*.[201]

One of the characteristics of Tommy Steele is that, with the exception of the unpleasant Charles Spencer and the stage hands at the London Palladium, everyone seemed to warm to him: Davies writing for the Wolverhampton Express and Star thought him 'easy going.[552] Farndale found him 'friendly and entertaining.'[553] He conveyed a youthful innocence bridging a gap between young and old. Tresidder found him 'courteous without a trace of flashiness.'[554] Ellis noted that he was the only rock 'n' roll singer known and liked by people in all walks of life.[555] Mitchell quotes a description of him as a young star: 'He is Pan, he is Puck, he is every nice young girl's boyfriend, every kid's favourite elder brother, every mother's cherished adolescent son.'[556] MacInnes (who transparently really liked and admired Tommy) believed that Steele's rise to 'the status of national idol' was only partly about his talent: he thought him both 'animally sensual' and yet 'innocent', possessing a 'joie de vivre' that he thought 'irresistibly engaging:'[557] he also saw him as 'like an elf, a sprite a faun from the forest.'[558] MacInnes saw him as very serious young man: one who spoke quietly but with great assurance, a young man with a great professional conscience.

One thing that really stirred the emotions of stuck-up intellectuals was his dress. He baffled the critics with

---

[201] The emigration of highly qualified people to be better off overseas

his tendency to do stage shows wearing jeans and casual shirts. The critics could not understand the appeal of an entertainer appearing onstage *not* dressed in a suit.[559]

Richardson quotes Paul Lincoln[202] remarking that Tom's success opened up new opportunities for youngsters like him. As he put it, his success encouraged agents to sign other teenagers for bill-topping honours. These other newcomers need to thank Tommy: he paved the way; he was the pioneer towards the new frontier of this new trend in entertainment. Lincoln put his finger on an important and essential truth. It is fashionable today for pundits to rubbish Tommy Steele and his early music: they do so at their peril. To do so is neither reasonable or fair. Without Tommy Steele (and the domestic market for rock 'n' roll that he brought about) it can be argued that none of the other stars who followed would have made it at all. The whole pop industry as it is today owes a great debt to this particular pioneer who, in his time and place, was truly the teenage idol of millions.[560]

His success helped to pave the way for other pre-Beatles rock 'n' roll idols from Cliff Richard to Billy Fury.[561] Beyond that, through the prodigious earnings he generated for Larry Parnes, he helped finance the Parnes Shillings and Pence 'Stable[203] of Stars:' enabling them to flourish[562] indirectly making an enormous contribution to the overall economic development of British rock 'n' roll.

---

[202] Part-owner of the 2is coffee bar when Tommy was discovered.
[203] MacInnes referred to Parnes écurie – and we cannot be at all certain that the reference was meant kindly

Tommy Steele made only a small number of really good rock records; his real importance is that his career served as a prototype for all the other English rockers.[563] In fact, he was the creator of an informal sort of blueprint for British rock 'n 'roll stardom:[564] an art form followed by almost every would-be teen idol who followed him: including the Beatles. Putting it another way, Marty Wilde, Cliff Richard, Adam Faith, the great Billy Fury (and all the other members of Larry Parnes' famous stable) might have made the big time – and then again some of them might not – but they all followed the trail blazed by Tommy Steele: and he deserves more credit for it than he has been given. So also does Kennedy who promoted him. Sandbrook (not one who writes overly kindly about Tommy Steele) remarks that he was the first domestic star to excite real passion among teenage followers and that the scenes at his concerts anticipated the shrieking bedlam that greeted the Beatles in 1963.[565] That is an understatement: ask those who were at the Globe in Stockton in 1957 (or indeed the Caird Hall in 1958).

Mitchell[566] opines that one must not overlook the fact that much of what Steele did was 'unique and pioneering' and that a great deal of his early success was due to his own determination to be perceived as a uniquely talented figure both on and off the stage. This might have led to some of the accusations of arrogance.

The notes for the brochure an *Evening with Tommy Steele* comment that his early days were pioneering. As Tommy said: "It was the first time that rock 'n' roll had been seen in Britain: because it was never seen before you could not make any mistakes." Undoubtedly, he played a key part in leading a new era in which rock 'n' roll became a new art form: one which he loved but was himself glad to leave behind. As Frame expressed it, he was the self-taught renaissance man of rock'n'roll.[567]

Let the last word rest with Frances Hardy who graciously suggested that it would not be preposterous to rate Sir Tommy Steele as Bermondsey's answer to Noël Coward himself.[568] A great compliment to a British polymath who, in his time and place, was the best-known entertainer in Britain (and Scandinavia!).

BIBLIOGRAPHY

[1] Mitchell, Gillian A.M: *A Very 'British' Introduction to rock 'n' roll: Tommy Steele and the Advent of rock 'n' roll Music in Britain, 1956–1960,* Contemporary British History, Vol. 25, 2011, Issue 2
[2] Mitchell, *op. cit.*
[3] Everitt, Don: *The Golden Boy Next Door*, John Bull, 31st May 1958
[4] Ellis, Royston: *The Big Beat Scene*, Four Square, 1961
[5] McAleer, Dave: *Hit Parade Heroes*, Hamlyn, 1993, p.26
[6] McAleer, *op. cit.* p.26
[7] Frame, Pete: *The Restless Generation*, Rogan House, 2007, p.435
[8] Mitchell, *op. cit.*
[9] Everitt, *op. cit.*
[10] Everitt, *op. cit.*
[11] Mitchell, *op. cit.*
[12] Steele, Tommy: *Bermondsey Boy*, Michael Joseph, 2006, p.238
[13] *An Evening with Tommy Steele,* souvenir brochure, July 1986
[14] Steele, Tommy: *My Own Story*, Pemrow Publications, undated, but 1957, p.39
[15] Smurthwaite, Nic; *Scene Stealer*, The Stage, 7th November 2005
[16] Bermuda News, 1st January 2011
[17] MacInnes, 1959, op cit
[18] Frame, Pete: *op. cit.* p.141
[19] Steele Tommy: *My Own Story, op. cit.* p.38
[20] *An Evening with Tommy Steele: op. cit.*
[21] Steele, Tommy: *Bermondsey Boy, op. cit.* p.235
[22] Stafford, David and Caroline; *The Lionel Bart Story*, Omnibus Press, 2011, p.40
[23] Napier-Bell, Simon; *You don't have to say you love me*, Ebury Press, New Edition, 2005
[24] Steele, Tommy: *Bermondsey Boy, op. cit.* p.235
[25] Tommy Steele: My Own Story, *op. cit.* p.22
[26] Tommy Steele: My Own Story, *op. cit.* p.50
[27] https://history-is-made-at-night.blogspot.com/2008/11/gyre-gimble-coffee-house-london-1950s.html
[28] Frame, Pete: *op. cit.* p.138
[29] Miles, Barry; *London Calling: A Countercultural History of London 1945*, Atlantic Books, 2011
[30] Stafford, *op. cit.* p.44
[31] Frame, Pete: *op. cit.* p.146
[32] Steele, Tommy: Bermondsey Boy, *op. cit.* p.240

33 Stafford, *op. cit.* p.44
34 Steele, Tommy: Bermondsey Boy, *op. cit.* p.241
35 Steele, Tommy: Bermondsey Boy, *op. cit.* p.237
36 The History of Rock, publication details unknown, p.129
37 Stafford, David and Caroline; *op. cit.* p.46
38 Napier-Bell; *op. cit.* 2005
39 Frame, *op. cit.* p.463
40 Frame, *op. cit.* pp.129/130
41 Miles, *op. cit.*
42 Frame, *op. cit.* p.142/3
43 Stafford, *op. cit.* p.46
44 Rogan, *op. cit* p.16
45 http://www.leodis.net/playbills/item.asp?ri=200391_99230594
46 The History of Rock, *op. cit.* p.130
47 Frame, *op. cit.* p.142
48 Frame, *op. cit.* p.144
49 Frame, *op. cit.* p.206
50 Ellis, *op. cit.* p.23
51 Tommy Steele Society, Newsletter #25, 2015
52 *The cult of Tommy Steele*, The Guardian, 11th June 1957
53 Everitt, Don: *op. cit.*
54 MacInnes, Colin; *The Mum's Delight*, Sunday Times Magazine, 1962
55 Rogan, *op. cit.* p.18
56 *An Evening with Tommy Steele, op. cit.*
57 Stafford, *op. cit.* p.49
58 Frame, *op. cit.* p.146
59 Everitt, op. cit.
60 http://www.spencerleigh.co.uk/2013/05/tommy-steele/
61 http://www.spencerleigh.co.uk/2013/05/tommy-steele/
62 Frame, *op. cit.* 2007
63 http://www.spencerleigh.co.uk/2013/05/tommy-steele/
64 Everitt, *op. cit.*
65 Mitchell, *op. cit.*
66 Frame, *op. cit.* p.474
67 McAleer, *op. cit.* p.26
68 Stafford, *op. cit.* p.120
69 Holt, Vickie; *Before the Invasion,* Blue Suede Shoes News, #69, Winter 2004. pp.5-9
70 Rogan, *op. cit.* p.19
71 Frame, *op. cit.* p.149

[72] Tommy Steele Society, Newsletter #22, 2014
[73] Frame, *op. cit.* p.144
[74] Stafford, *op. cit.* p.66
[75] Stafford, *op. cit.* p.80
[76] Everitt, *op. cit.*
[77] McAleer, *op. cit.* p.90
[78] Tommy Steele Society, Newsletter #1, July 2007
[79] McAleer, *op. cit.* p.27
[80] Tatham, Dick; *Vocal Views by Dick Tatham*, Record Mirror, 9th February 1957
[81] Rogan, Johnny: *Starmakers and Svengalis*, Macdonald Queen Anne Press, 1988, p. 17
[82] Holt, *op. cit.* pp.5-9
[83] Rogan, Johnny: *op. cit.* p.17
[84] Rogan, *op. cit.* p.18
[85] *The cult of Tommy Steele*, Manchester Guardian, 11th June 1957
[86] Napier-Bell, *op. cit.*
[87] Frame, *op cit.* p.145
[88] Frame, *op. cit.* pp.147-9
[89] Sandbrook, Dominic; *Never had it so good*, Little Brown, 2005
[90] Kennedy, John: *Tommy Steele*, Souvenir Press, 1958
[91] Tommy Steele: *My Own Story*, *op. cit.* p.21
[92] Exhibition at Powysland Museum, May-September 2006, Curator's Briefing Notes
[93] Steele, Tommy: Bermondsey Boy, *op. cit.* p.250
[94] http://www.bigredbook.info/article4.09.html
[95] Frame, *op, cit.*
[96] https://books.google.co.uk/books?id=CbWrDwAAQBAJ&pg=PT235&lpg=PT235&dq=tommy+steele+chiswick+empire&source=bl&ots=CDk9Hw14wD&sig=ACfU3U1XBFfQvEQo0yh6P3VBLAM-vwEu3w&hl=en&sa=X&ved=2ahUKEwjq07Wt-ZnmAhX6RhUIHe-vD_I4ChDoATAMegQICBAB#v=onepage&q=tommy%20steele%20chiswick%20empire&f=false
[97] Steele, Tommy: *Bermondsey Boy, op. cit.* p.252
[98] http://www.yorkshirefilmarchive.com/film/northern-life-tommy-steele-returns-sunderland-empire
[99] https://books.google.co.uk/books?id=nB2KDwAAQBAJ&pg=PA194&lpg=PA194&dq=tommy+steele+%2B+bristol+hippodrome+1957&source=bl&ots=z8c6twGysH&sig=ACfU3U2buPnonTtlLiC9YC8ZrSGS6CJUIg&hl=en&sa=X&ved=2ahUKEwiX0I7PupzmAhVPUBUI

HZl6AoU4ChDoATABegQIChAB#v=onepage&q=tommy%20steele%20%2B%20bristol%20hippodrome%201957&f=false

[100] Cummings, J; *Rock 'n' Roll Again.* Sunderland Echo, 6th November 1956

[101] https://books.google.co.uk/books?id=5-SaAwAAQBAJ&pg=PT193&lpg=PT193&dq=reg+thompson+comedian&source=bl&ots=jyTuBQ7H-9&sig=ACfU3U1maeA9Cy1ao_KDCxWY7KKIzPGS9Q&hl=en&sa=X&ved=2ahUKEwiOiaqV0pnmAhXCVRUIHdYUA5kQ6AEwDHoECAsQAQ#v=onepage&q=reg%20thompson%20comedian&f=false

[102] Frame, *op. cit.* p.150

[103] *The cult of Tommy Steele, op. cit.*

[104] Steele, Tommy: *Bermondsey Boy*, op. cit.

[105] Melody Maker, 8th December 1956, p.8

[106] Bragg, Billy: *Roots, Radicals and Rockers: How Skiffle Changed the World,* Faber, 2017

[107] The Guardian, 10th December 1963

[108] Steele, Tommy Steele: *My own story*, *op. cit.* p.37

[109] https://books.google.co.uk/books?id=EtBe7a_WtlgC&pg=PT102&lpg=PT102&dq=Major+Donald+Neville-Willing&source=bl&ots=b7H503ev74&sig=ACfU3U0niIzr24F8aE8C2VszWuimldrZdA&hl=en&sa=X&ved=2ahUKEwintJSLtpLmAhWlmFwKHQznDmcQ6AEwBnoECAcQAQ#v=onepage&q=Major%20Donald%20Neville-Willing&f=false

[110] Massingberd, Hugh: *Sorry guv this cockney act won't wash,* Daily Mail, 15th October 2006

[111] Kent Messenger, 20th December 1956

[112] The History of Rock, *op. cit.* p.131

[113] Ellis, *op. cit.* p.58

[114] McAleer, *op. cit.* p.27

[115] McAleer, *op. cit.* p.26

[116] Stafford, *op. cit.* p.46

[117] https://www.alamy.com/jan-01-1957-britains-rock-n-roll-idol-meets-south-african-beauty-queen-image69343931.html

[118] Hardy, Frances: *The First Pop Star*, The Daily Mail, 26th August 2006

[119] Steele, Tommy: *Bermondsey Boy, op. cit.* p.270

[120] https://www.imdb.com/title/tt1804332/

[121] http://www.tvpopdiaries.co.uk/1957.html

[122] Kynaston, *op. cit.* p.10

[123] Kynaston, *op. cit.* p.11
[124] Ellis, *op. cit.*
[125] Lashua B, Spracklen K. and Wagg S: *Sounds and the City: Popular Music, Place and Globalization*, Springer, 2014
[126] Steele, Tommy: *Bermondsey Boy*, *op. cit.* p.259
[127] Stafford, *op. cit.* p.52
[128] Nunn, Ray; *Face to Face with Tommy Steele*, Woman's Mirror, 21st September, 1963
[129] http://www.turnipnet.com/whirligig/tv/adults/rocknroll/sixfivespecial.htm
[130] http://www.tvpopdiaries.co.uk/1957.html
[131] http://www.spencerleigh.co.uk/2013/05/tommy-steele/2/
[132] Frame, *op. cit.* p.150
[133] Stafford, *op. cit.* p.452
[134] The cult of Tommy Steele, *op. cit.*
[135] McAleer, *op. cit.* p.90
[136] Stafford, *op. cit.* p.52
[137] Frame, *op. cit.* p.251
[138] http://www.tvpopdiaries.co.uk/1957.html
[139] Fife Today, 8th February, 2018
[140] MacInnes, *op. cit.*
[141] hhttp://www.spencerleigh.co.uk/2013/05/tommy-steele/2/ https://www.telegraph.co.uk/news/obituaries/sport-obituaries/9309422/Frank-Parr.html
[142] Judt, Tony: *Postwar: a History of Europe since 1945*, Penguin, 2005, p.349
[143] https://genome.ch.bbc.co.uk/schedules/bbchomeservice/basic/1957-04-22
[144] Exhibition at Powysland Museum, *op. cit.*
[145] Obituary*: Freddie Bell: 'Giddy-Up-A Ding Dong' singer*, 13th February, The Independent, 2008
[146] https://www.burtonlatimer.info/industry/coles-boot-co.html
[147] Heath, Doug: www.ourglasgowstory.com 12.01.05
[148] Frame, *op. cit.*, p.257
[149] Laing, Dave: The Guardian, 15th February 2008
[150] https://funeral-notices.co.uk/national/death-notices/notice/Freddie+Bell/2192772
[151] Ellis, *op. cit.* p.90
[152] Lark, Claire: *Barry Band: Drum roll please... but keep it down as*

Britain's very first rock 'n' roller Tommy Steele crashes into resort, Blackpool Gazette, 15th February 2020

[153] *The cult of Tommy Steele, op. cit.*
[154] Webster, Jack: *Jack Webster's Aberdeen*, Birlinn, 2007, p.179
[155] Tommy Steele Society, Newsletter #32, 2017
[156] Tommy Steele Society, Newsletter #1, July 2007
[157] Tommy Steele Society, Newsletter #17, 2012
[158] Stafford, *op. cit.* p.53
[159] Tommy Steele Society, Newsletter #1, July 2007
[160] Farndale, Nigel: *I just want my mum to love me,* Daily Telegraph, 17th August 2015
[161] Bjorn, Claus, Bjorke, Bo and Sevaldsen, Jørgen: *Britain and Denmark: Political, Economic and Cultural Relations in the 19th and 20th centuries,* Museum Tusculanum Press, 2003, p.503
[162] https://www.alamy.com/aug-08-1957-tommy-steeles-mum-moves-out-of-her-bermondsey-home-to-image69347452.html
[163] DISC, 1961
[164] https://www.britishpathe.com/video/tommy-gets-moving/query/tommy+steele
[165] https://www.google.com/search?q=tommy+steele+home+in+catford+1957&rlz=1C1CHBF_en-GBGB874GB874&sxsrf=ACYBGNQk_IL6ZJCamFA2U6gA4jPyDSEPFQ:1575140479066&tbm=isch&source=iu&ictx=1&fir=QrR9gjnKqcauOM%253A%252CFZYYQBRvvQalvM%252C_&vet=1&usg=AI4_-kQ7njwMw1ZaWKfgpkmhtBvGI58q-A&sa=X&ved=2ahUKEwjAmufFz5LmAhUTlFwKHaSvCRgQ9QEwC3oECAkQBg
[166] Frame, *op. cit.* p.472
[167] Frame, *op. cit.* p.482
[168] The Tommy Steele Society, Newsletter #14, November 2011
[169] *An Evening with Tommy Steele,* souvenir brochure, July 1986
[170] https://www.svd.se/svds-recension-av-tommy-steeles-legendariska-konsert
[171] Exhibition at Powysland Museum, *op. cit.*
[172] Larsen, Charlotte Rørdam: *Above all it's because he's English: Tommy Steele and the Notion of Englishness as Mediator of Wild Rock 'n' Roll, Britain and Denmark*: Political, Economic and Cultural Relations in the 19th and 20th Centuries, Museum Tusculanum, 2003
[173] Everitt, *op. cit.*
[174] Tommy Steele Society, Newsletter #2, November 2007

[175] Billboard, 7th April
[176] Nygaard, Bertel, *The High Priest of Rock and Roll: The Reception of Elvis Presley in Denmark, 1956–1960*, Popular Music and Society, 2018
[177] Mäkelä, Janne, *John Lennon Imagined: Cultural History of a Rock Star,* Peter Lang, 2004, p.32
[178] Nielsen, JØRGEN; Skovvej; *When the rock came to Aarhus,* JYLLANDS-POSTEN Aarhus, 12th April 2008
[179] Bjorn, Claus, Bjorke, Bo and Sevaldsen, Jørgen, *op. cit.*
[180] http://www.tvpopdiaries.co.uk/1957.html?LMCL=GMuHFE
[181] Melody Maker, September 28th 1957
[182] Stafford, *op. cit. p.*56
[183] Steele, Tommy: *Bermondsey Boy, op. cit.* p.294
[184] Steele, Tommy: *Bermondsey Boy, op. cit.* p.296
[185] Steele, Tommy: *Bermondsey Boy, op. cit.* p.259
[186] The Tommy Steele Society, Newsletter #17, November 2012
[187] Mitchell, *op. cit.*
188 Mitchell Gillian A. M; *Adult Responses to Popular Music and Intergenerational Relations in Britain*, c. 1955–1975, Anthem, 2019
[189] http://www.spencerleigh.co.uk/2013/05/tommy-steele/2/
190 Higgins, Susan; *Conversations with Ann Howard*, AuthorHouse UK, 2014, p.14
[191] Farndale, *op. cit.*
[192] http://www.spencerleigh.co.uk/2013/05/tommy-steele/2/
[193] Tommy Steele Society, Newsletter #1, July 2007
[194] Tommy Steele Society, Newsletter #23, 2014
[195] Mitchell, *op. cit.*
[196] http://www.tvpopdiaries.co.uk/1958.html
[197] http://www.spencerleigh.co.uk/2013/05/tommy-steele/2/
[198] http://www.tvpopdiaries.co.uk/1958.html
[199] https://www.alamy.com/feb-02-1958-tommy-steele-leaves-for-south-africa-by-boat-because-of-image69349867.html
[200] The Tommy Steele Society, Newsletter #2, November 2007
[201] Stafford, *op. cit.* p.53
[202] Hamm, Charles: *Putting popular music in its place*, Cambridge University Press, 1995, p.153
[203] Hamm, Charles: op. cit.
204
https://www.britishpathe.com/video/VLVAAXS3T308HICZI6L23U02ZAXHW-SOUTH-AFRICA-TOMMY-STEELE-ARRIVES-FOR-SOUTH-AFRICAN-TOUR/query/COBALT

[205] https://www.britishpathe.com/video/VLVAAXS3T308HICZI6L23U02ZAXHW-SOUTH-AFRICA-TOMMY-STEELE-ARRIVES-FOR-SOUTH-AFRICAN-TOUR/query/COBALT
[206] Cape Times, March 1958
[207] Holt, *op. cit.* pp.5-9
[208] MacInnes, *op. cit.*
[209] Mitchell, *op. cit.*
[210] Mitchell, *op. cit.*
[211] https://www.britishpathe.com/video/VLVA12O7SR94FNT4AESQFUVD3R0LJ-SOUTH-AFRICA-SIR-TOMMY-STEELE-CAPETOWN/query/tommy+steele
[212] http://www.spencerleigh.co.uk/2013/05/tommy-steele/3/
[213] Frame, *op. cit.* p.305
[214] https://en.wikipedia.org/wiki/Bantu_Men%27s_Social_Centre
[215] http://www.historicalpapers.wits.ac.za/inventories/inv_pdfo/AG2887/AG2887-A5-14-002-jpeg.pdf
[216] The Tommy Steele Society, Newsletter #24, March 2015
[217] Holt, *op. cit.* pp. 5-9
[218] http://www.ministryofrock.co.uk/tommysteele.html
[219] https://www.facebook.com/251922131233/posts/on-record-60th-anniversary-of-tommy-steeles-south-african-tour-1958-2018mvfb-tom/10155780765441234/
[220] McAleer, *op. cit.* p.31
[221] http://www.bigredbook.info/article4.09.html
[222] https://arkiv.dk/soeg?searchString=Koncert%20med%20Tommy%20Steele%20i%20Fyens%20Forum%201958&arkiv=234
[223] The Tommy Steele Society, Newsletter #2, November 2007
[224] Frame, *op. cit.* p.307
[225] http://www.spencerleigh.co.uk/2013/05/tommy-steele/3/
[226] Farndale, *op. cit.*
[227] https://www.bbc.co.uk/programmes/b007tdvy
[228] Strachan, Graeme; *Let me go. The night Britain's first teen idol Tommy Steele was almost torn apart in Dundee,* The Courier, 30th April 2018
[229] Disc, 24th May 1958
[230] Steele, Tommy: Bermondsey Boy, *op. cit.* p.261
[231] Stanley, Bob: *How Tommy Steele, Britain's biggest pin-up, was*

savaged by the teenage mob, The Times, 16th July 2018
[232] Madera Tribune, Volume 67, #22, 12th June 1958
[233] https://www.br.de/radio/bayern2/sendungen/kalenderblatt/2009-tommy-steele-erster-rock-n-roll-musiker-wachsfigur-madame-tussauds-100.html
[234] Everitt, *op. cit.*
[235] http://www.spencerleigh.co.uk/2013/05/tommy-steele/2/
[236] Mitchell, *op. cit.*
[237] Frame, *op. cit.* p.306
[238] http://www.spencerleigh.co.uk/2013/05/tommy-steele/3/
[239] Stafford, *op. cit.* p.86
[240] https://ohboy.org.uk/tv-series/diary/november
[241] Kynaston, *op. cit.* p.194
[242] Holt, *op. cit.* pp. 5-9
[243] The Tommy Steele Society, Newsletter #2, November 2007
[244] Mitchell, *op. cit.*
[245] Steele, Tommy: *Bermondsey Boy*, *op. cit.* p.296
[246] The Tommy Steele Society, Newsletter #24, March 2015
[247] *Tommy Explains the New Mr Steele*, NME, 1963
[248] Steele, Tommy: *Bermondsey Boy*, *op. cit.* p.296
[249] Kynaston, *op. cit.* p.261
[250] Smurthwaite, op. cit.
[251] https://genome.ch.bbc.co.uk/page/313d25410da442f9a5d7d31c995df4ed
[252] Cleland, Gary; The Daily Telegraph, 22nd April 2008
[253] https://www.imdb.com/title/tt4562382/
[254] http://www.tvpopdiaries.co.uk/1959.html?LMCL=Z1f3MF
[255] https://ohboy.org.uk/tv-series/diary/november
[256] Sunday Graphic, undated, 1959
[257] Steele, Tommy: *Bermondsey Boy*, *op. cit.* p.302
[258] Frame, *op. cit.* p.404
[259] Frame, *op. cit.* p.405
[260] Stafford, *op. cit.* p.84
[261] Stafford, *op. cit.* p.84
[262] Stafford, *op. cit.* p.85
[263] Stafford, *op. cit.* p.85
[264] https://www.theguardian.com/news/2013/aug/04/observer-archive-tommy-steele-moscow
[265] https://www.theguardian.com/news/2013/aug/04/observer-archive-tommy-steele-moscow
[266] https://www.facebook.com/BBCArchive/videos/1959-newsreel-

tommy-steele/631779197195114/
[267] Eder, Bruce: https://www.allmusic.com/ /tommy-steele-mn0000515856/biography
[268] https://en.wikipedia.org/wiki/Juke_Box_Jury
[269] Perry, Chris: *The Kaleidoscope British Christmas Television Guide 1937-201,* Kaleidoscope Publishing; 2nd Revised Edition, 2016
[270] https://www.aboutmyarea.co.uk/Hampshire/Portsmouth/PO6/Days-Gone-By/Nostalgia/89189-The-Wonderful-World-of-Billy
[271] http://www.tvpopdiaries.co.uk/1959.html
[272] Petrie, Duncan; *Bryanston Films: An Experiment in Cooperative Independent Film Production and Distribution*, Historical Journal of Film, Radio and Television, 2017
[273] Frame, *op. cit.* p.405
[274] https://jukeboxjury.uk/category/programmes/bbc-juke-box-jury-1960/
[275] http://henryjenkins.org/blog/2019/11/10/promoting-tommy-steele-through-1950s-uk-comics-part-i-by-joan-ormrod
[276] https://www.thetimes.co.uk/article/how-tommy-steele-britains-biggest-pin-up-was-savaged-by-the-teenage-mob-rsdvt6xzt
[277] *Tommy Steele signs for £100,000 tour*, unnamed newspaper, 1959
[278] http://www.spencerleigh.co.uk/2013/05/tommy-steele/2/
[279] http://www.tvpopdiaries.co.uk/1960.html
[280] *We myde ya, and we can break ya,* LIFE, 2nd July 1965
[281] Tommy Steele Society, Newsletter #3, March 2008
[282] *2,000 fans scream for Tommy*, Sunday Express, 19th June 1960
[283] The Observer: *profile: Tommy Steele*
[284] Ellis, *op. cit.* p.61
[285] *Steele reveals four-year secret*, DISC, late 1960
[286] *Steele reveals four-year secret, op. cit.*
[287] Johnson, Derek; *Tommy Steele's Lumkin (sic) mesmerises audience,* NME, November, 1960
[288] *We myde ya, and we can break ya; op. cit.*
[289] *Dick Whittington,* souvenir brochure notes, 1969
[290] Nevin, Charles, The Independent, 13th March 1994
[291] Best, Betty: *Tommy Stoops to conquer,* Australian Women's Magazine, 21st December 1960
[292] Purcell, Hugh: *A very private celebrity*, The Robson Press, 2015, p.157
[293] The Tommy Steele Society, Newsletter #25, July 2015

²⁹⁴ *Steele gets mediaeval show for ATV*, NME, December 1960
²⁹⁵ *Fewer records for Mr Steele*, DISC, 1961
²⁹⁶ https://www.gettyimages.co.uk/detail/news-photo/president-of-bermondsey-boat-club-tommy-steele-relaxes-at-news-photo/993668996
²⁹⁷ NME, 1961, undated
²⁹⁸ The Tommy Steele Society, Newsletter #4, July 2008
²⁹⁹ *Tommy Steele TV* – June 25, DISC, 1961
³⁰⁰ http://www.eafa.org.uk/catalogue/97932
³⁰¹ *Tommy's missed hit*, Daily Express, November 1961
³⁰² https://www.alamy.com/nov-11-1961-sid-james-risks-his-life-at-stars-guy-fawkes-party-a-fireworks-image69396415.html
³⁰³ The Daily Mail, 15th March 2006, no by-line
³⁰⁴ Knightley, Philip and Kennedy, Caroline; *An Affair of State*, Jonathon Cape, 1987, pp.48-49
³⁰⁵ https://thelatest.co.uk/brighton/2013/11/05/52691/
³⁰⁶ The Tommy Steele Society, Newsletter #4, July 2008
³⁰⁷ The History of Rock, *op. cit.* p.131
³⁰⁸ http://www.tvpopdiaries.co.uk/1962.html
³⁰⁹ Tatham, Dick; *Tommy Steele explains that eleven-month break from discs.* DISC, c.1962
³¹⁰ Nunn, Ray; *Face to Face with Tommy Steele*, Woman's Mirror, 21st September, 1963
³¹¹ Henshaw, Laurie; *Steele attacked on Jury*, Melody Maker, 1962
³¹² http://www.tvpopdiaries.co.uk/1962.html
³¹³ Wilson, A. N; *Betjeman*, Hutchinson, 2006, p.255
³¹⁴ Winter Gardens Bournemouth, programme notes, 12th August, 1962
³¹⁵ McHugh, Dominic: *Oxford Handbook of Musical Theatre Screen Adaptions,* Oxford Handbooks, 2019
³¹⁶ http://www.tvpopdiaries.co.uk/1963.html?LMCL=SC7_Gd
³¹⁷ *Singer quits rehearsal to give evidence*, The Daily Telegraph, February 1963
³¹⁸ NME, 22nd March 1963
³¹⁹ Hobson, Sir Harold: The Sunday Times, March 1963
³²⁰ Shorter, Eric: The Daily Telegraph, March 1963
³²¹ https://www.wimbledonsw19.com/#.pages/wimbledonsw19:info:tommysteeleinwimbledon002
³²² https://www.spectator.co.uk/2013/01/when-the-yankees-came/
³²³ McHugh, *op. cit.*
³²⁴ McHugh, *op. cit.*

[325] NME, 31st May 1963
[326] *Royal Box for Blind Woman*, The Daily Telegraph, undated
[327] The Daily Telegraph, 1963
[328] https://www.alamy.com/jun-18-1963-18-6-63-tommy-steele-banned-from-driving-takes-to-bike-image69405334.html
[329] https://www.wsc.co.uk/the-archive/95-Miscellaneous/4656-the-showbiz-xi
[330] http://www.richardmmills.com/
[331] https://missingepisodes.proboards.com/thread/11849/richard-whittington-esquire-tommy-steele
[332] https://www.wimbledonsw19.com/#.pages/wimbledonsw19:info:tommysteeleinwimbledon002
[333] McHugh, *op. cit.*
[334] https://www.tvobscurities.com/2016/07/tv-guide-ad-alcoa-preview/
[335] Tommy Steele Society, Newsletter #6, March 2009
[336] *We myde ya, and we can break ya; op. cit.*
[337] Hammond, Peter: NME, late 1961
[338] McHugh, *op. cit,* p.574
[339] Los Angeles Times, 22nd November, 1965
[340] Newark Evening News, 26th April, 1965
[341] *We myde ya, and we can break ya: op. cit.*
[342] https://showbox.space/tv-show/the-ed-sullivan-show/season/18/episode/36
[343] The Daily Express, 4th October 1965
[344] Exhibition at Powysland Museum, *op. cit.*
[345] Saunders, Tristram Fane; 4th November 2016
[346] McHugh, *op. cit.* p.574
[347] https://www.imdb.com/title/tt0061749/trivia?ref_=tt_trv_trv
[348] McHugh, *op. cit.*
[349] Oxford Mail, 25th November 2013
[350] Stafford, *op. cit.* p.195
[351] NME, 11th November 1966
[352] https://www.walesonline.co.uk/lifestyle/nostalgia/how-mike-bernie-winters-led-11185895
[353] Tommy Steele Society, Newsletter #6. March 2009
[354] http://my1960s.com/tv-and-film/the-heart-of-show-business/
[355] https://en.wikipedia.org/wiki/The_Happiest_Millionaire
[356] http://www.markrobinsonwrites.com/the-music-that-makes-me-dance/2015/9/23/disneys-dud-the-happiest-millionaire
[357] https://www.latimes.com/archives/la-xpm-1999-jul-29-ca-60536-

story.html
[358] Desert Sun, Volume 39, #311, 3rd August 1966
[359] Desert Sun, 9th August 1967
[360] Desert Sun, Volume 41, #61, 14th October 1967
[361] McHugh, *op. cit.*
[362] https://www.rogerebert.com/reviews/half-a-sixpence-1968
[363] McHugh, *op. cit.*
[364] https://genome.ch.bbc.co.uk/schedules/bbcone/london/1968-02-04
[365] http://www.spencerleigh.co.uk/2013/05/tommy-steele/3/
[366] Lewisohn, Mark: *The Beatles - All These Years*; Extended Special Edition: Volume 1, Little Brown, 2013
[367] https://www.empireonline.com/movies/reviews/finians-rainbow-review/
[368] https://www.rogerebert.com/reviews/finians-rainbow-1968
[369] The Tommy Steele Society, Newsletter #6, March 2009
[370] http://www.screenonline.org.uk/tv/id/1136314/index.html
[371] http://www.screenonline.org.uk/tv/id/527251/index.html
[372] https://conradbrunstrom.wordpress.com/2017/03/24/the-1969-tv-adaptation-of-twelfth-night-guinness-plowright-richardson-and-yes-tommy-steele/
[373] https://www.britishtheatreguide.info/reviews/dvd-12thnight-rev
[374] Everitt, *op. cit.*
[375] https://letterboxd.com/film/wheres-jack/
[376] http://collections.vam.ac.uk/item/O86189/tommy-steele-in-ithe-servant-caricature-sommerlad-gilbert/
[377] Billington, Michael; *Left Hungry for more*, The Guardian, 18th December 1999
[378] The Sun, February 1969
[379] The Daily Sketch, February 1969
[380] Interview for Northampton Chronicle and Echo, 30th January 2004
[381] https://genome.ch.bbc.co.uk/00b2739d33ce4937a31b38a93805e8ae
[382] The Tommy Steele Society, Newsletter #7, 2009
[383] The Tommy Steele Society, Newsletter #9, March 2010 *(letter from Mike Moseley)*
[384] https://www.standard.co.uk/home/celebs-on-the-move-7225031.html
[385] Clifford, Max and Levin, Angela: *Max: Read All About It*, Virgin, 2005
[386] https://www.britishpathe.com/video/special-lord-mayors-show
[387] The Tommy Steele Society, Newsletter #7, 2009
[388] John Barber, The Daily Telegraph, December 1969

[389] The Tommy Steele Society, Newsletter #7, 2009
[390] https://www.gettyimages.co.uk/detail/news-photo/english-entertainer-tommy-steele-witha-troupe-of-dancers-at-news-photo/603390821
[391] http://beat-magazine.co.uk/2018/tommy-the-rock-n-roller-who-became-britains-premier-song-and-dance-man
[392] Las Vegas Sun, February 1971
[393] Exhibition at Powysland Museum, *op. cit.*
[394] Billboard, 6th June 1970
[395] Billboard, 2nd June 1973
[396] http://beat-magazine.co.uk/2018/tommy-the-rock-n-roller-who-became-britains-premier-song-and-dance-man
[397] The Tommy Steele Society, Newsletter #7, 2009
[398] Hischak, Thomas S; *Disney Voice Actors: A Biographical Dictionary,* Performing Arts, 2011
[399] https://www.imdb.com/title/tt1379126/
[400] https://forums.digitalspy.com/discussion/1447767/tommy-steele-sequel-to-cinderella
[401] http://www.arthurlloyd.co.uk/DudleyTheatres.htm
[402] http://cinematreasures.org/theaters/41631
[403] The Tommy Steele Society, Newsletter #7, 2009
[404] https://www.wearebarnsley.com/news/2153/we-are-barnsley-dj-set-to-celebrate-milestone
[405] Michael Parkinson Meets Tommy Steele, BBC One, 22nd September 1979
[406] Tommy Steele: *What a Show!* souvenir brochure, 1994
[407] Mitchell, *op. cit.*
[408] Tommy Steele: *What a Show*! *op. cit.*
[409] http://beat-magazine.co.uk/2018/tommy-the-rock-n-roller-who-became-britains-premier-song-and-dance-man
[410] *Shaggy dog stories: From Tommy Steele's terrier and a stolen greyhound to a burglar's lookout and a bona fide war hero*, The Daily Mail, 12th June 2010
[411] The Tommy Steele Society, Newsletter #8, November 2009
[412] Napier-Bell, *op. cit.*
[413] Shaw, Karen: Northern Life, 6th October 2011
[414] https://www.coventrytelegraph.net/incoming/gallery/day-old-photos-taken-coventry-11845423
[415] http://www.richardmmills.com/1972-1986.html
[416] http://www.richardmmills.com/1972-1986.htm
[417] http://gasdisc.oakapplepress.com/yeolfest.htm
[418] http://gasdisc.oakapplepress.com/yeolfest.htm

[419] https://www.gettyimages.co.uk/detail/news-photo/english-entertainer-tommy-steele-pretends-to-be-decapitated-news-photo/844077786
[420] The Tommy Steele Society, Newsletter #8, 2009
[421] https://forums.digitalspy.com/discussion/2130555/thames-television-on-this-day-1978/p3
[422] The Tommy Steele Society, Newsletter #9, March 2010
[423] http://timworthington.blogspot.com/2016/12/christmas-with-childrens-itv-quincys.html
[424] http://www.richardmmills.com/1972-1986.htm
[425] https://www.celebrityspeakers.com.au/michael-edgley/
[426] *Australian Tommy Steele Show*, souvenir brochure. 1982
[427] http://www.richardmmills.com/1972-1986.html
[428] http://www.overthefootlights.co.uk/London%20Revues%201970-1979.pdf
[429] Mitchell, *op. cit.*
[430] http://www.downthelane.net/extras/2007/10/04/an-evening-with-tommy-steele/
[431] The Tommy Steele Society, Newsletter #9, March 2010
[432] https://books.google.co.uk/books?id=C5hIB9rdT7sC&pg=PT348&lpg=PT348&dq=an+evening+with+tommy+steele+prince+of+wales+theatre&source=bl&ots=ERAzdBWyG7&sig=ACfU3U0jhUXBDlPF4ZQB9kT_qufiDXkqZw&hl=en&sa=X&ved=2ahUKEwjYu-e50f7nAhWToFwKHSG2CAo4HhDoATABegQIChAB#v=onepage&q=an%20evening%20with%20tommy%20steele%20prince%20of%20wales%20theatre&f=false
[433] https://genome.ch.bbc.co.uk/search/500/20?order=desc&q=%22Maggie+Philbin%22&svc=9371541
[434] https://genome.ch.bbc.co.uk/1ec895218bdc4481930c31a151118b3e
[435] The Daily Mail, 13th May 1981
[436] Riley, Joe; Arts Editor, Liverpool Echo, October 1981
[437] Farnhill, Barrie; Yorkshire Post, 28th November 1981
[438] https://www.gettyimages.co.uk/detail/news-photo/prince-charles-meets-vera-lynn-and-tommy-steele-at-a-news-photo/914811876
[439] Frame, *op. cit.* p.435
[440] https://www.liverpoolecho.co.uk/incoming/gallery/look-back-christmas-liverpool-through-6361267
[441] http://www.trashfiction.co.uk/final_run.html
[442] Desert Sun, #39, 19th September 1983

443 https://www.dresscircle.london/singin-in-the-rain-original-london-cast-cd-5229-p.asp
444 Corliss, Richard; *Singin' in the Rain Is Back: What a Glorious Feeling.* Time, 12th July 2012
445 Sweet, Matthew: *Singin' in the Rain, Sadler's Wells, London; A wonderful feeling? No, not exactly,* The Independent, 8th August 2004
446 Tommy Steele Society, Newsletter #10, July 2010
447 Churcher, Sharon: *Still Kicking,* New York Magazine, 14th October 1985
448 https://www.whatsonstage.com/london-theatre/reviews/singin-in-the-rain_17024.html
449 Boon, Maxine; *Review: Singin' in the rain (Australian tour),* Limelight, 17th May 2016
450 Spencer, Charles; *Singin' in the Rain, Chichester Festival Theatre, Review,* 6th July 2011
451 Nevin, Charles; *op. cit.*
452 Johns, Ian; *The Raining Champion,* The Times, 26th July 2004
453 Hobson, Sir Harold; The Sunday Times, 1983
454 Bristol Evening Post, 1985
455 King, Francis; The Daily Telegraph, 1983
456 Oh, The Catholic Herald, 1983
457 Frame, *op. cit.* p.436
458 https://www.boatingbusiness.com/news101/industry-news/farewell_earls_court
459 https://www.gettyimages.co.uk/photos/jimll-fix-it?mediatype=photography&phrase=jim%27ll%20fix%20it&sort=best
460 The Tommy Steele Society, Newsletter #10, July 2010
461 http://bufvc.ac.uk/tvandradio/ilrsharing/index.php/segment/1250 (Accessed 10 Mar 2020)
462 https://www.bradford-theatres.co.uk/news/archive/alhambra-theatre-in-bradford-celebrates-100-glorious-years
463 Tommy Steele, *What a Show!* souvenir brochure
464 Exhibition at Powysland Museum, *op. cit.*
465 Tommy Steele Society, Newsletter #10, July 2010.
466 https://visitbristol.co.uk/blog/read/2018/04/the-historic-bristol-marriott-royal-hotel-celebrates-150-years-b789
467 The Tommy Steele Society, Newsletter #10, July 2010
468 *Singin' in the Rain,* 1989 souvenir brochure
469 Harold Fielding Ltd, Company Notes for Japanese Tour, 1987

[470] https://en.wikipedia.org/wiki/Flying_Tiger_Line
[471] *Tokyo Weekender*, 27th March 1987
[472] Morgan, Fergus; *Company stage manager Zac Holton: 'This is the easiest job in the world and the most difficult'*, The Stage, 6th May 2019
[473] The Tommy Steele Society, Newsletter #10, July 2010
[474] Stage and Television Today, 17th March 1988
[475] The Independent, 21st July 2018
[476] Desert Sun, 18th May 1988
[477] Nightingale, Benedict; New York Times, 11th August 1988
[478] Nightingale, *op. cit.*
[479] Rayment, Tim: *Touch of Steele puts a new spring in the old Ziegfeld routine*, The Sunday Times, 22nd May 1988
[480] http://www.overthefootlights.co.uk/London%20Musicals%201989%20New.pdf
[481] *Some Like it Hot*, souvenir programme, 1991
[482] Tommy Steele, *What a Show! op. cit.*
[483] Manchester Evening News, 16th August 1991
[484] Southern Evening Echo, 1991
[485] Tresidder, Megan; *How Steele Evolved from the Caveman*, Sunday Times, 23rd February 1992
[486] http://www.overthefootlights.co.uk/London%20Musicals%201992%20New.pdf
[487] The Times, March 1992
[488] Nevin, *op. cit.*
[489] The Daily Express, March 1992
[490] https://books.google.co.uk/books?id=nLGpBAAAQBAJ&pg=PT146&lpg=PT146&dq=Bermondsey+Boy+statue+Rotherhithe&source=bl&ots=TBewn6z0yK&sig=ACfU3U2noZW9ZGBVBfepI8Fo3eBBc58UiA&hl=en&sa=X&ved=2ahUKEwjarcG8i-_nAhWUh1wKHVj5DpI4FBDoATAHegQICRAB#v=onepage&q=Bermondsey%20Boy%20statue%20Rotherhithe&f=false
[491] http://museu.ms/event/details/116632/twickenham-stadium-arts-tour
[492] Nevin, *op. cit.*
[493] Exhibition at Powysland Museum, *op. cit.*
[494] Smurthwaite, *op. cit.*

495 Hardy, *op. cit.*
496 https://www.oldies.com/artist-biography/Tommy-Steele.html
497 Nevin, *op. cit.*
498 Shuttleworth, Ian; Financial Times, 1995
499 Tommy Steele Society, Newsletter #11, November 2010
500 Exhibition at Powysland Museum, *op. cit.*
501 Somerset County Gazette, 4th September 2003
502 The Daily Telegraph, May 1999
503 The Tommy Steele Society, Newsletter#11. November 2010
504 http://www.hoadly.co.uk/html/theatre_main.htm?LMCL=fUduw8
505 The Tommy Steele Society, Newsletter #10, March 2011
506 https://www.youtube.com/watch?v=rzg0sj61cKo
507 http://archive.southwark.anglican.org/thebridge/0104/page07.htm
508 https://www.liverpoolecho.co.uk/news/liverpool-news/liverpools-eleanor-rigby-statue-vandalised-17113415
509 Mandrake, Sunday Telegraph, 2006
510 Overbury, Karen; The Journal, 28th October 2010
511 https://thelatest.co.uk/brighton/2013/11/05/52691/
512 *Tarantino eyes Tommy Steele*, The Evening Standard, 21st April 2004
513 Meakin, Nione: The Argus, 14th December 2013
514 Frame, *op. cit.* p,140
515 Mitchell, *op. cit.*
516 https://openplaques.org/plaques/10416
517 *Gillian Reynolds' Choices,* Daily Telegraph, October 2006,
518 Shenton, Mark; *Thoughts on a fellow critic as Charles Spencer bows out*, The Stage, 2nd September 2014
519 The Tommy Steele Society, Newsletter #18, March 2013
520 *Scrooge*, programme notes, Winter 10/11
521 Key, Phil; Liverpool Daily Post, 14th November 2007
522 Review of *Dr Dolittle*, www.indieLondon.co.uk, 12th November 2007
523 The Tommy Steele Society, Newsletter #9, March 2010
524 *About my area*, 9th December 2009
525 The Tommy Steele Society, Newsletter #10, March 2011
526 Munro, David: *quoted* in the Tommy Steele Society, Newsletter #10, March 2011
527 Review of *Scrooge*, www.indielondon.com 22nd October 2010
528 Fryer, Jane; *Two-mile runs every day, hours on the tennis court and bouncing around in a West End show that keeps him up until 3am: How Tommy Steele is still rocking at 81 in The Glenn Miller*

Story, Daily Mail, 29th July 2018
[529] https://www.rbhistory.org.uk/about-us
[530] https://www.bbc.co.uk/programmes/b0188f9w
[531] Barking and Dagenham Post, 2nd August 2013
[532] Interview with *Female First*, 17th February 2016
[533] https://www.wimbledonsw19.com/#.pages/wimbledonsw19:info:tommysteeleinwimbledon002
[534] http://www.spencerleigh.co.uk/2013/05/tommy-steele/2/
[535] https://www.thereviewchap.blogspot.com.thereviewchap.com/2018/08/the-glenn-miller-story-tommy-steele.html
[536] Wiegand, Chris: *Andrew Lloyd Webber unveils Wall of Fame at London Palladium,* The Guardian, 15th October 2018
[537] https://www.facebook.com/282967823195/posts/tommy-steele-lunch-with-tommy-in-attendancethursday-7th-november-2019lansdowne-c/10156517438723196/
[538] Press Association, 7th November 2019
[539] MacInnes, Colin; Profile Tommy Steele, Elizabethan, 1959
[540] Nunn, *op. cit.*
[541] Riddell, Mary; *Rock on Tommy,* Daily Mail Magazine, 2006
[542] Disc, late autumn 1960
[543] MacInnes, *op. cit.*
[544] Riddell, *op. cit.*
[545] Mitchell, *op. cit.*
[546] Holt, *op. cit.* pp. 5-9
[547] Smurthwaite, *op. cit.*
[548] Everitt, *op. cit.*
[549] MacInnes, *op. cit.*
[550] Frame, op. cit. p.435
[551] http://www.downthelane.net/extras/2007/10/04/an-evening-with-tommy-steele/
[552] Davies, Nina; Wolverhampton Express and Star, 13th February 2004
[553] Farndale, *op. cit.*
[554] Tresidder, *op. cit.*
[555] Ellis, *op. cit.*
[556] Mitchell, *op. cit.*
[557] MacInnes, *op. cit.*
[558] MacInnes, *op. cit.*
[559] Holt, *op. cit.* pp. 5-9

[560] Tommy Steele Society, Newsletter #1, July 2007
[561] Mitchell, *op. cit.*
[562] Frame, *op. cit.* p.435
[563] The History of Rock, *op. cit.* p.131
[564] Mitchell, *op. cit.*
[565] Sandbrook, *op. cit.* p.444
[566] Gillian *op. cit.*
[567] Frame, op. cit. p.150
[568] Hardy, *op. cit.*

Printed in Great Britain
by Amazon